ECLIPSE 2023

The Year 2023 World in Chaos

Deenagh Miller

Amazon.com

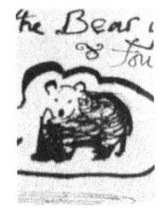

ISBN-13: 9798395447173
ISBN-10: 1477123456

Cover design by: Art Painter
Library of Congress Control Number: 2018675309
Printed in the United States of America

To all those artists of the past whose work I love more than I can say & who continue to influence my own work. Here are just a few:

Massacio
Ruebens
Rembrandt
Van Eyk
Girlandhiao
Vermeer
Giotto
Fra Angelico
Raphael
Chardin
Piero della Francesca
Veronese
Titian
Bosch
Michelangelo
Altdorfer
Sebastiano del Piombo
Blake
Leonardo da Vinci
Goya
Velasquez
Monet
Manet
Bruegel
Matthias Grunewald

CONTENTS

INTRODUCTION

'Eclipse Twenty Twenty Three'.

The action in this book takes place in the air, sea & on land against a background of stars, planets & clouds. I wanted to find & draw the reality between the real & the imagined, where the scale of people, objects, incidents, animals can vary dramatically.

It's impossible to explain or exactly define the imagination. I see it as both a personal & universal dimension, - a kind of daydreaming in which we can all participate - like an internet of the mind, but without the computer or mobile phone. It can also act as an antidote to the anxieties & fears we all suffer from at times.

I see the world as a moving picture to be drawn in pen & ink. Sometimes the pen leads, sometimes I do. It wouldn't stop after 'The Year 2020 World in Chaos' so I decided it had to leave aside the pandemic & politics & draw on imagination, memory, fantasy, & to see a different story evolve.
Veronese's Musician and the Dreaming Woman reappear on the frontispiece. In between them is an etching of a brain by Andreas Vesalius, 1514 - 1564, one of the first anatomists. His work was so controversial it was smuggled out of Italy.

A monkey holds a thread. A large fish prods him in the back. A clock hangs in space. Time, art, dreams, history, psychology, philosophy, science, introspection, interpretation, came to mind. 'Mankind hangs on a thread' said Carl Jung in an interview shortly before he died. His research into psychology stimulates & is still controversial.

I have many cut out images - of dancers, actors, plants, musicians, animals, insects, fish & or more, from newspapers, magazines, leaflets, catalogues & chose them like you might do from a pack of cards, by picking one from many.

Some pictures provoke questions, - can a mask mirror the persona we present to others, & also allude to the pitfalls of self deception? Does the man with the body of a horse looking over a woman playing the lyre provoke thoughts about relationships or romance?
Does the 'Ship of Fools' sailing in the long hair signify the folly & frailty of mankind?

Fewer words can attract more attention. I wanted the reader to be able to identify an individual page from the words alone, so the main contents of each page are described as simply & briefly as possible. The references are there to explain & encourage research into their meaning.

A picture can mean different things to different people, & meaning can change over time. It's not necessary to know a lot about art to ask oneself & others questions, - it will develop confidence in one's own ideas, thoughts, responses, & stimulate the imagination.

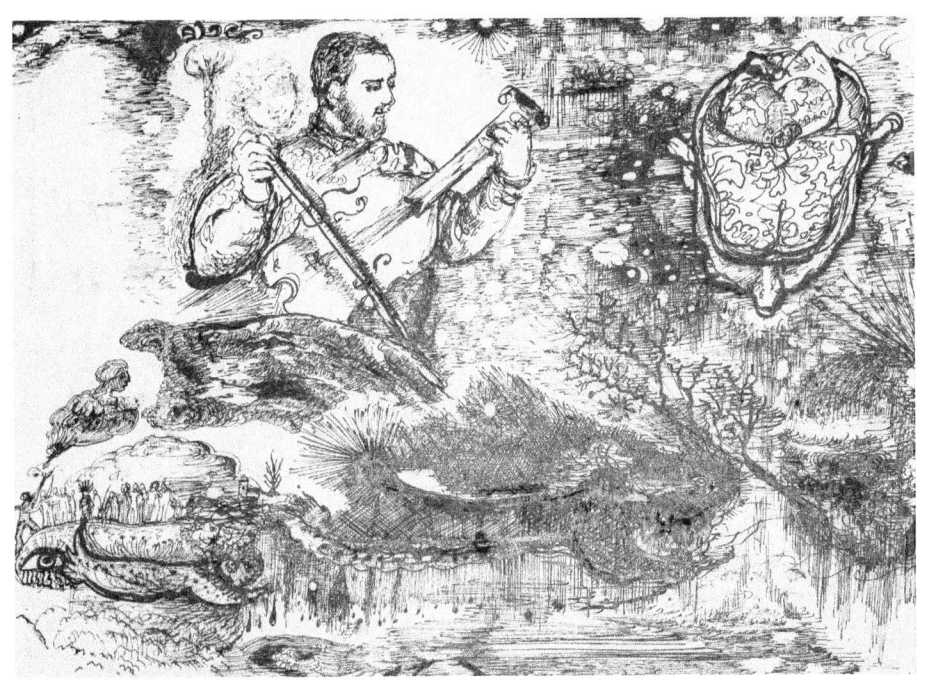

Frontispiece 1

Musician, from the painting 'The Marriage at Cana' by Paolo Veronese 1528 -1588. Known as the Venetian Painter.

For sheer beauty, colour, atmosphere & life enhancing feeling, he is the Impressionist of the Renaissance.

He was also a painter of myth & imagination.

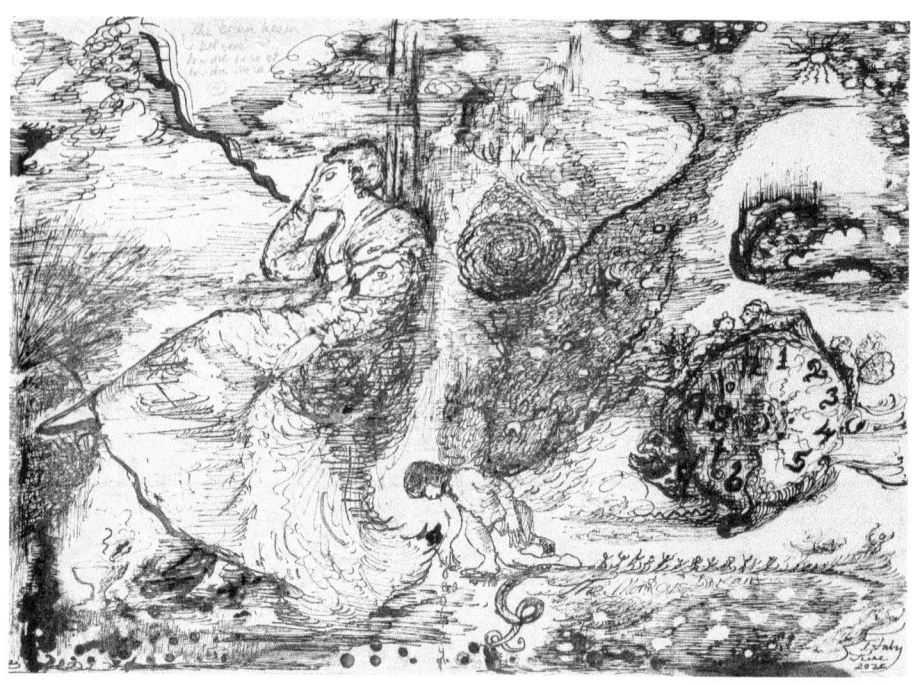

Frontispiece 2
Dreaming Woman from the 'Dream of St Helena' by Paolo
Veronese 1528 - 1588. Known as the Venetian Painter.
Superbly skilled as an artist, Veronese was also deeply insightful
& understanding of human nature & behaviour. Many of his
paintings include the lives & loves of the greatest & smallest
people.

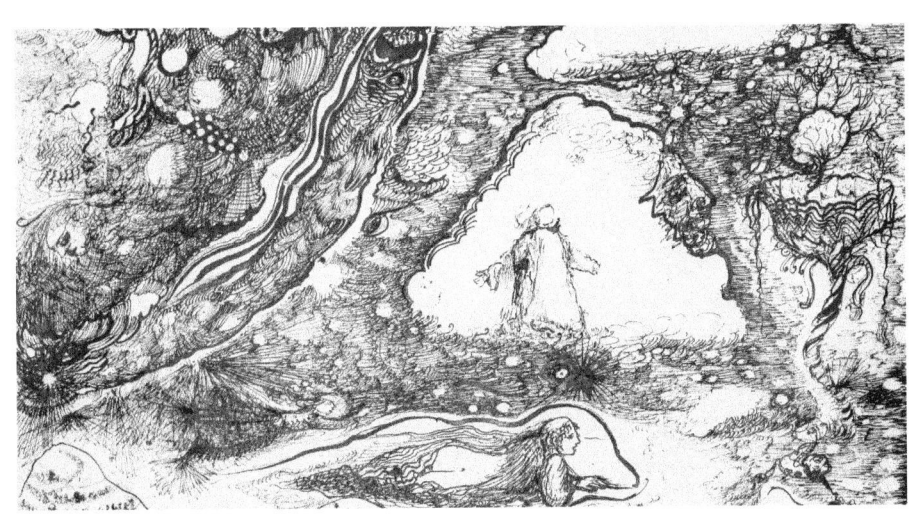

CHAPTER 1 HUMANS   IN TROUBLE

Humans are in Trouble. Tentatively I drew a planet or curtain drawn aside, revealing someone on their knees. Then, underneath, a small 'Tower of Babylon' appeared. What has overwhelmed, shocked, even awed this person? Is there a reason, an explanation?

Below, someone wakes up, what to?

The person is from Goya's 1814 painting, 'The Third of May 1808'.

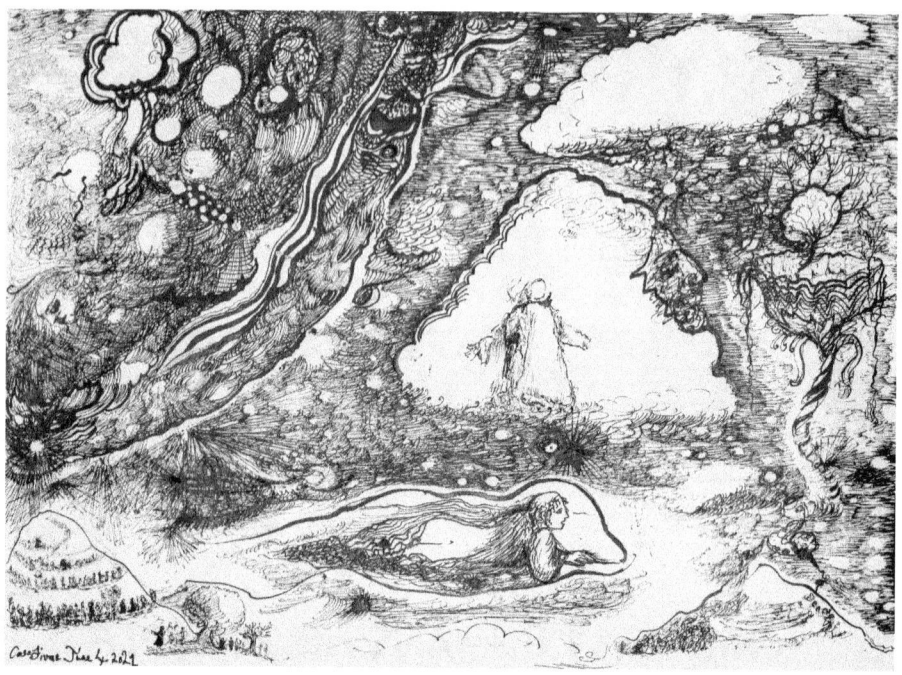

The words 'Humans are in Trouble' felt right for this chapter. How to make sense of the unsettling government lockdowns & vaccines, what would happen next I wondered?

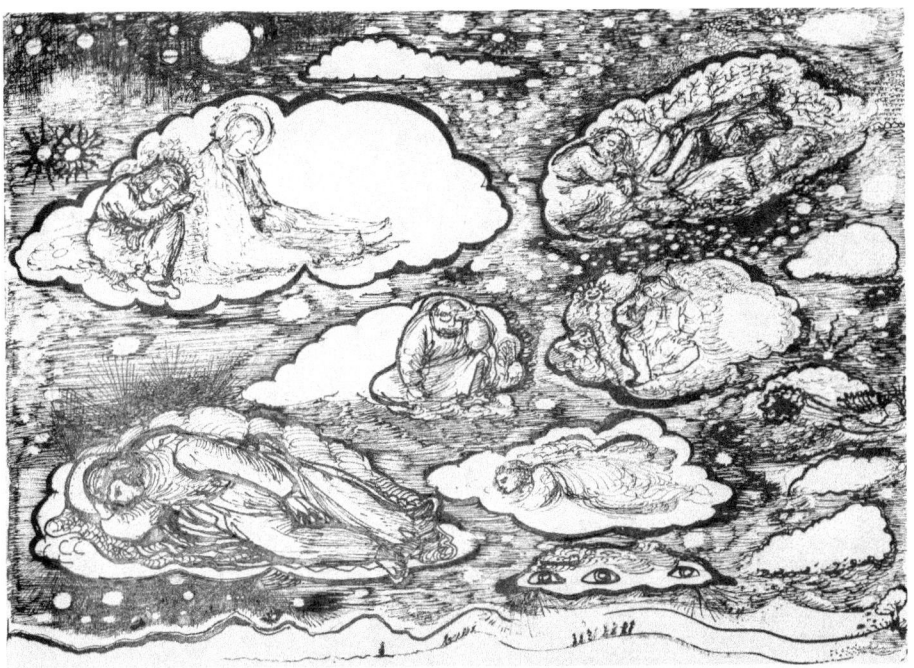

In a dark sky, inside six white clouds eight people are asleep. Is this what those from the previous page see? Who will wake? The sky has three eyes & below, tiny figures walking over distant hills. The sleepers are from Renaissance painters Giovanni Bellini 1430 - 1516 & Andrea Mantegna 1431 - 1506.

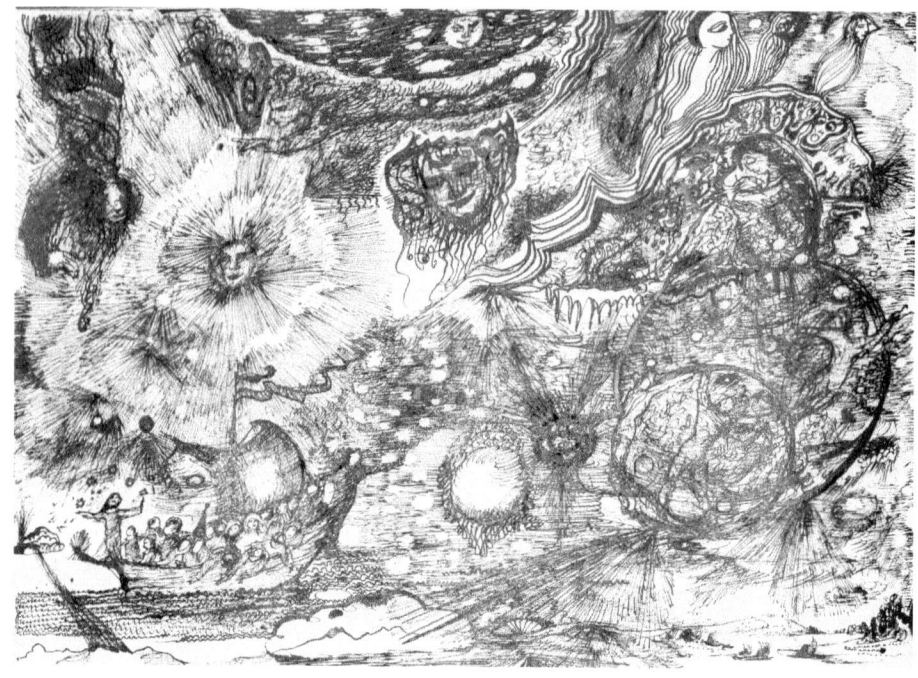

One face with many rays, odd others, many stars, something falling from space, a full 'Ship of Fools' sails across. Someone crouches on a planet, two others are inside, more rays, clouds, a distant landscape.

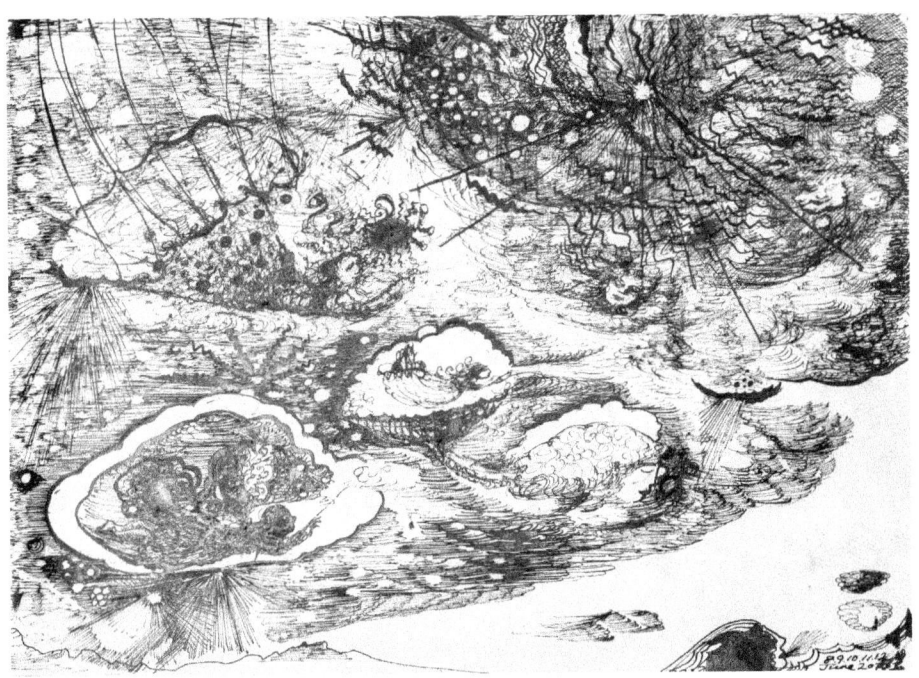

Against a striated sky, long lines radiate from a planet, various female figures, some in clouds & a profile fly at or past it. From the long dress of one, lines go to & fro from space.

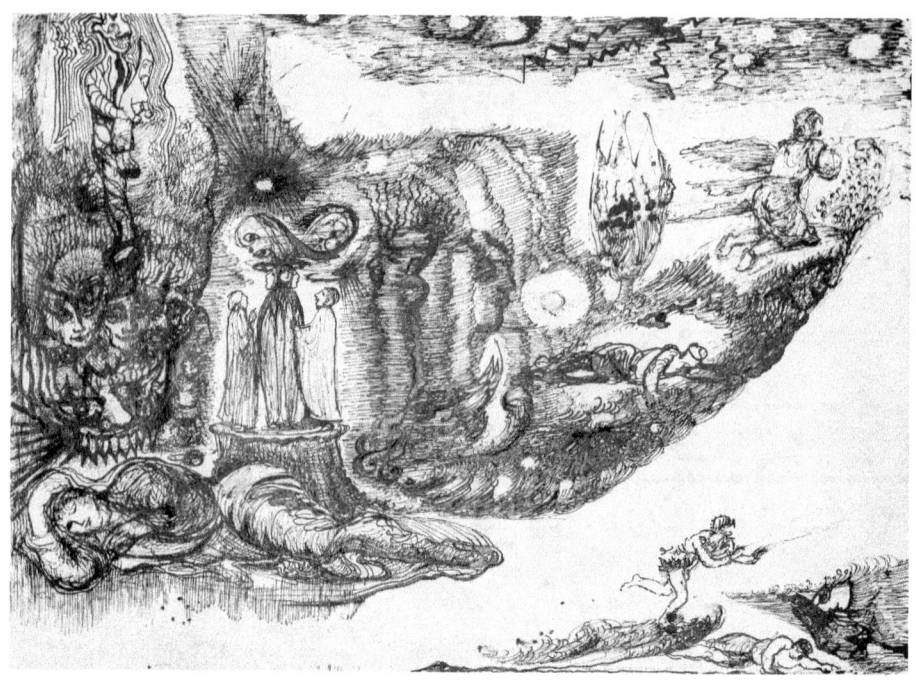

Under a strange stripy clown, three figures, one with a weird hat converse on a tree stump, witchy faces, a praying man from Bellini's 1459 painting 'Agony in the Garden' looks over the edge, another gropes below, a large person, arm overhead sleeps. Separate & lower still, overlooked by two lying profiles a man stumbles, the other crawls.

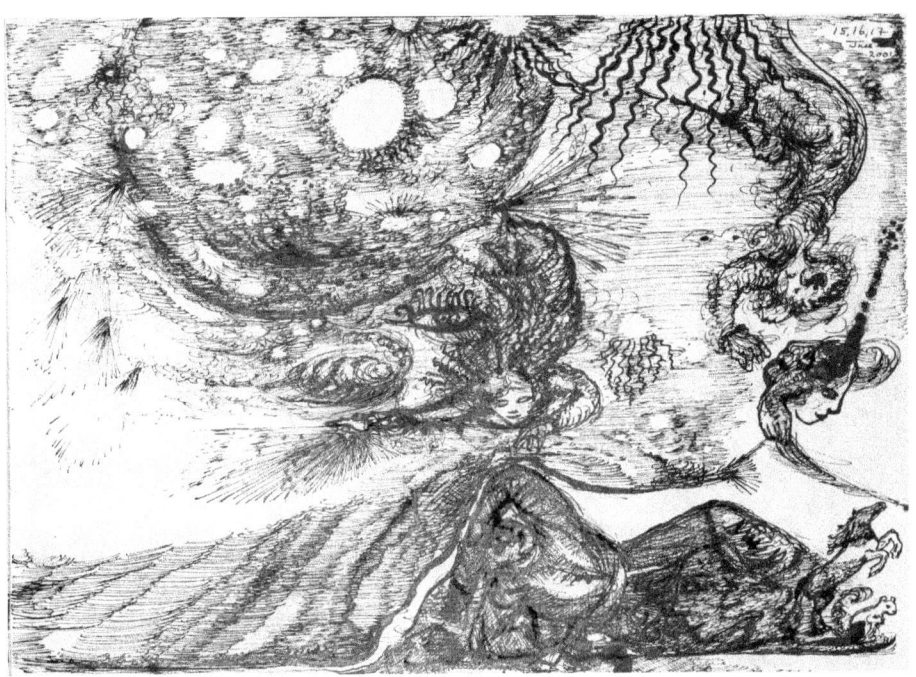

Rays issue from above a planet with craters, two females watched by an eye, spiral down, one touches a fissure of the earth to a trapped man near a horse rearing over a squirrel. The other female approaches a volcano spewing two heads.

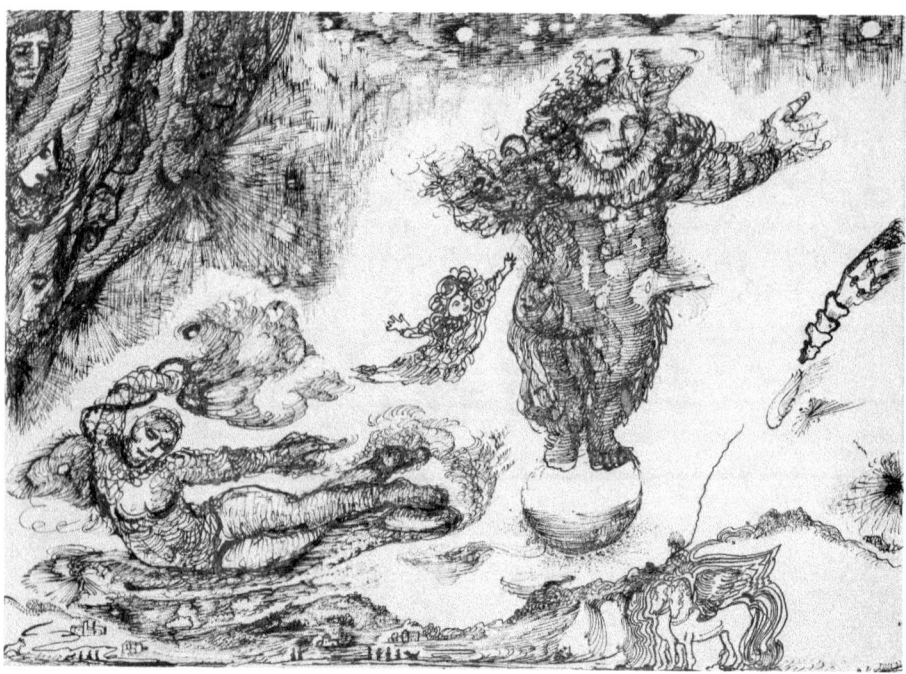

The curve of a planet bursts with tiered faces & rays. Beneath stars a one handed clown sleeps on an empty globe. A reclining woman raises a swirling arm, releasing clouds & a figure flying at the clown. Below are buildings, tiny people, two winged horses & just above, in the sky, the tip of a human spine leaving the page.

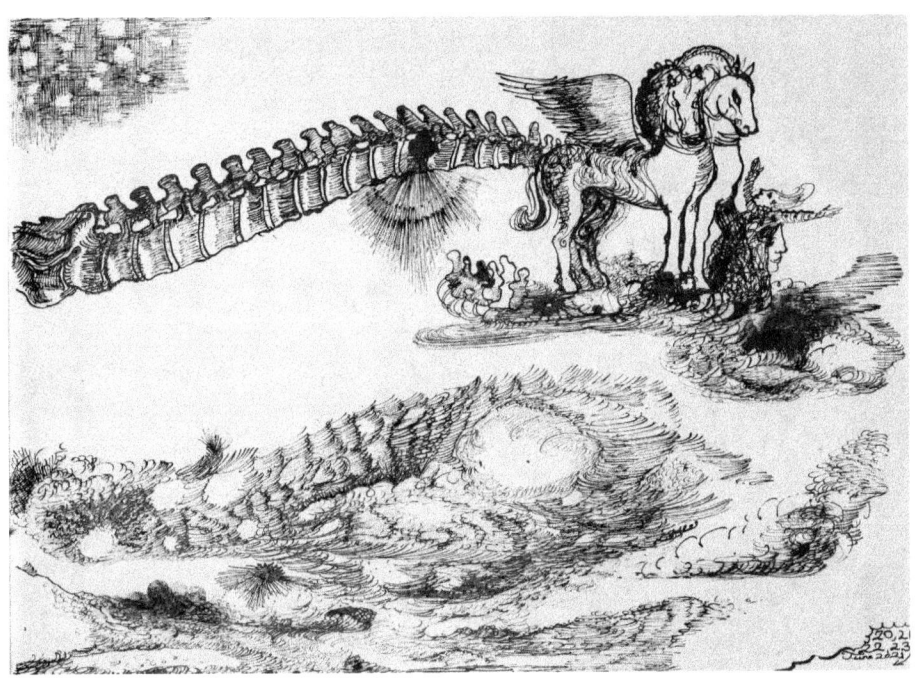

The spine from the previous page grows enormous & stops just behind two winged horses. A small human with a profile in its back reaches up to them. Below, clouds & land merge.

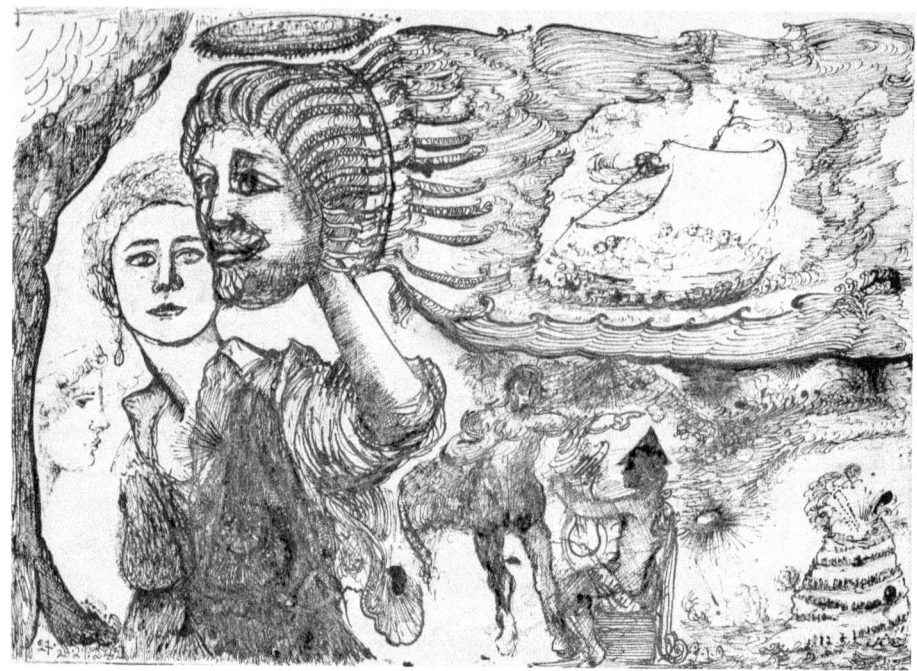

A young woman holds up a large mask, its hair flowing across both pages in which sails a 'Ship of Fools'. Near her, hangs a curtain & a profile. To her left a man with the body of a horse, is pointing over a woman playing the lyre - from 'The Education of Achilles' 1772 by James Barry. Nearby a crowd circles a Tower of Babylon to a volcano at the top. The mask is from a Puppetry performance of Theseus. Tobacco Factory, Bristol.

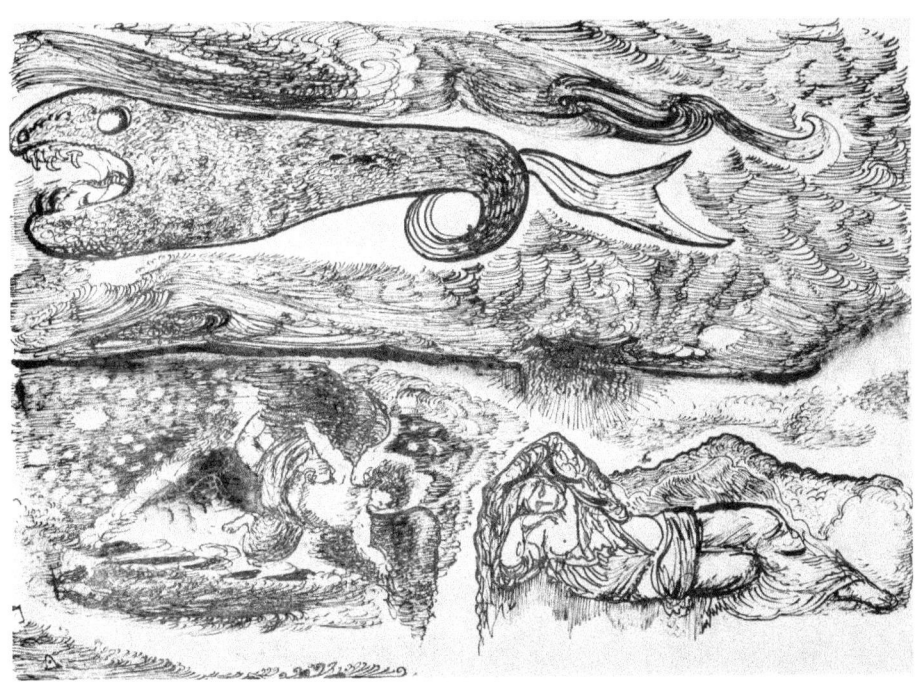

In the masked man's long hair, a giant fish prepares to swallow the 'Ship of Fools'. Below, a winged boy spirals from darkness towards a woman, reclining or sleeping with an arm over her head.

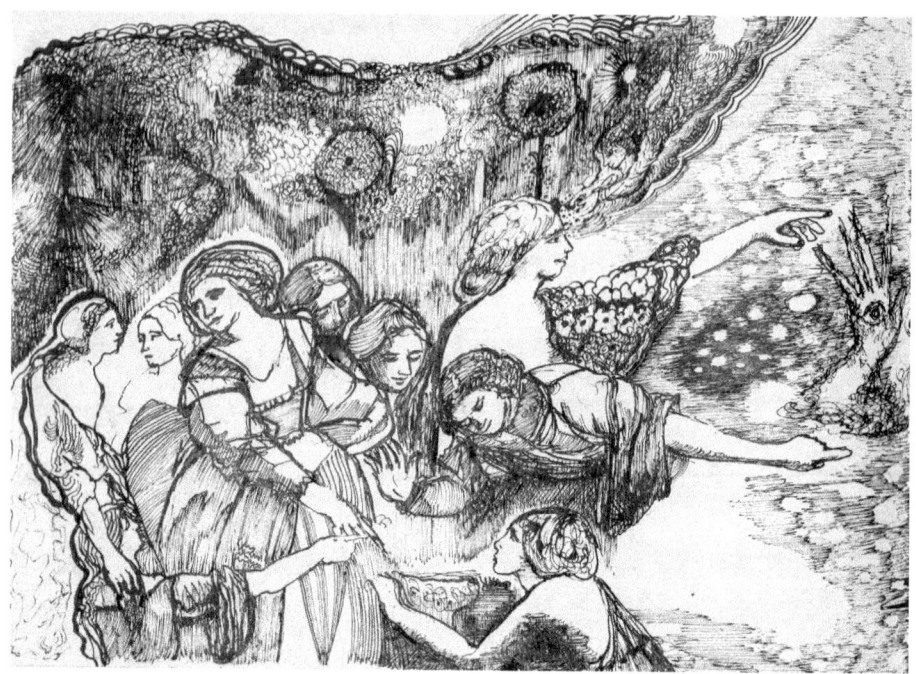

In front of a moth-shaped tapestry composed of plants is drawn the 1630 painting 'The Finding of Moses' by Orazio Gentileschi. However this young woman's basket is empty. Hands with eyes in their palms from the Spanish film 'Pan's Labyrinth', cover the centre of both pages.

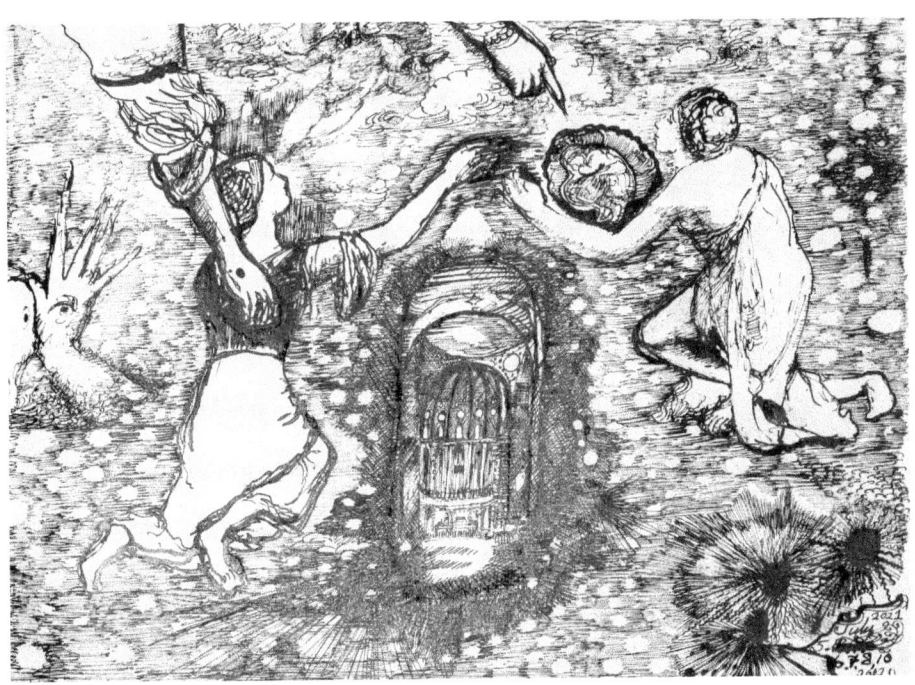

Stars pierce a dark sky where two young women from Finding Moses hover either side of the darkly drawn Basilica of St Anthony in Padua, Italy. A hand descends, touches one girl on the back, the other points to a basket with a sleeping girl.

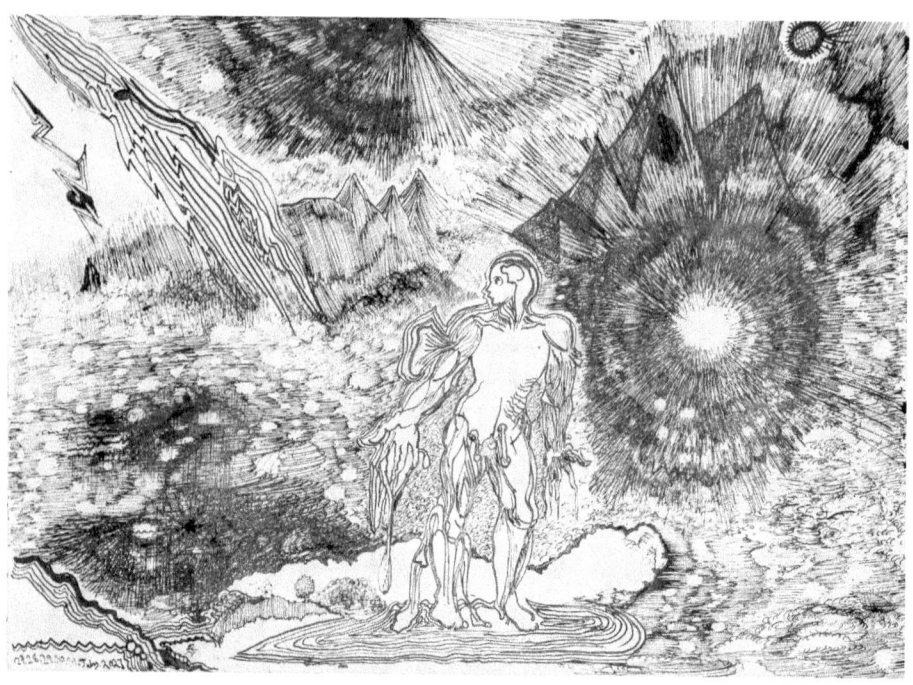

In a strange land, a young man stands alone on an island of circular lines. Has lightning hit him & what is he looking at? Behind mountains the sky is dark, rays emanate from a large hole.

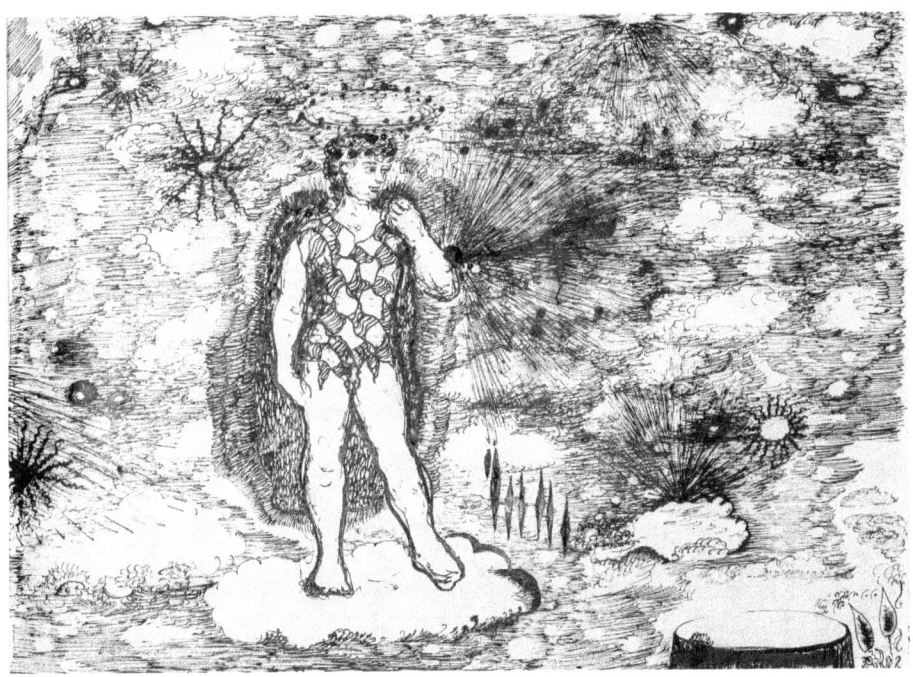

A solitary young man on a cloud with a halo overhead, wears a Harlequin outfit without leggings. Holding a cloak over his shoulder, he looks dreamily at a tree stump in the corner. From his elbow dark rays spread into a sky with stars, rays & seven long diamond shapes near his leg.

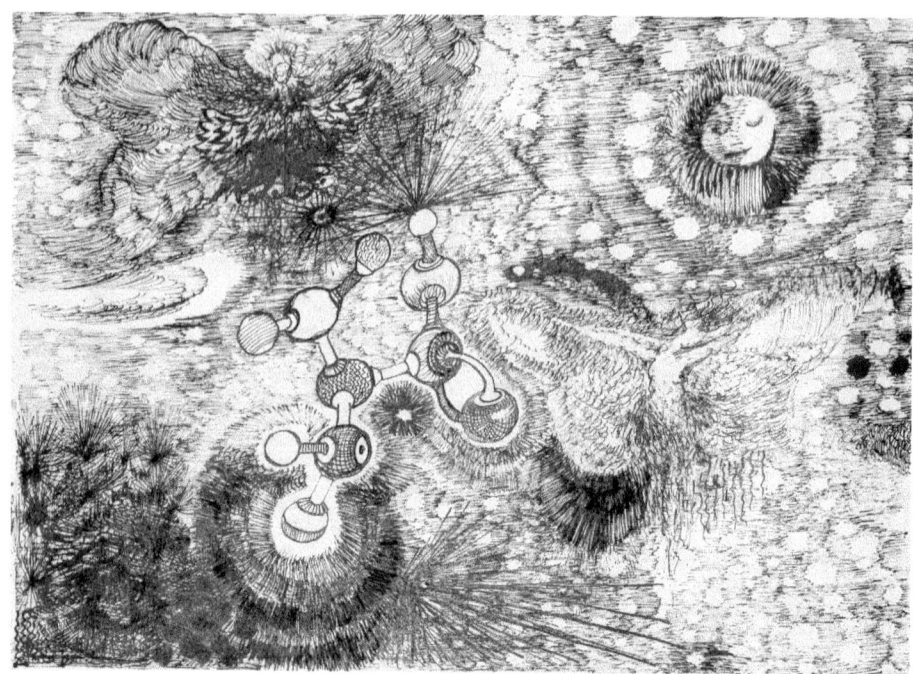

Bottom corner, an Open University Molecular Model from a 1990's Environmental Science Degree explodes into the sky. Two butterfly forms hover midair. A sun surrounded by holes, winks.

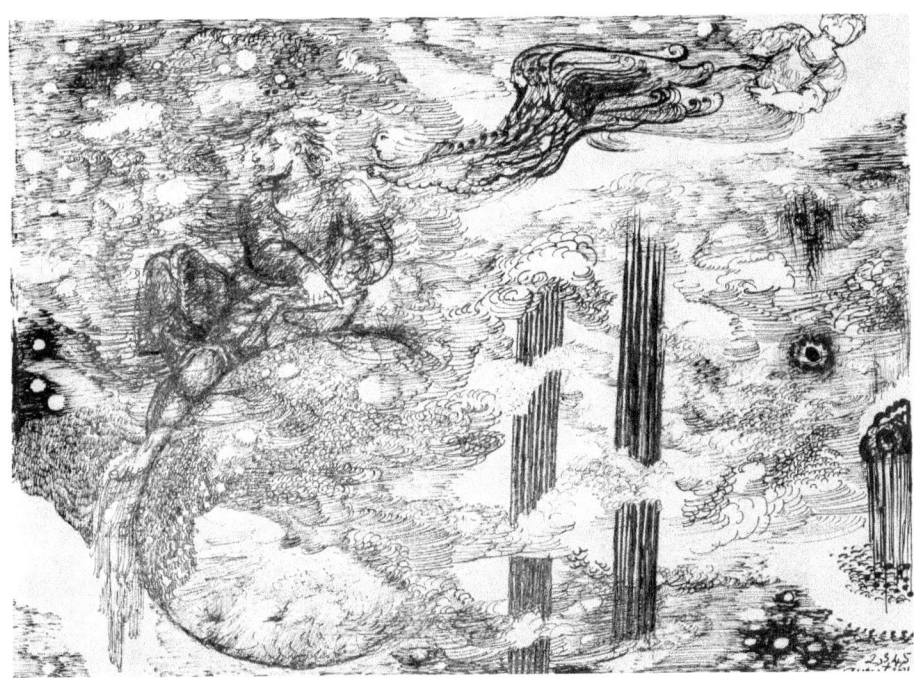

In a calm sky Sebastiano del Piombo's (Michelangelo's assistant) 'Prophet' painted for the Borgherini Chapel 1518, sits atop a planet, clutches a book, points downwards. Nearby, two columns rise, pierce clouds where a small black hole, & a sad face hover. In the upper corner someone flies from the page.

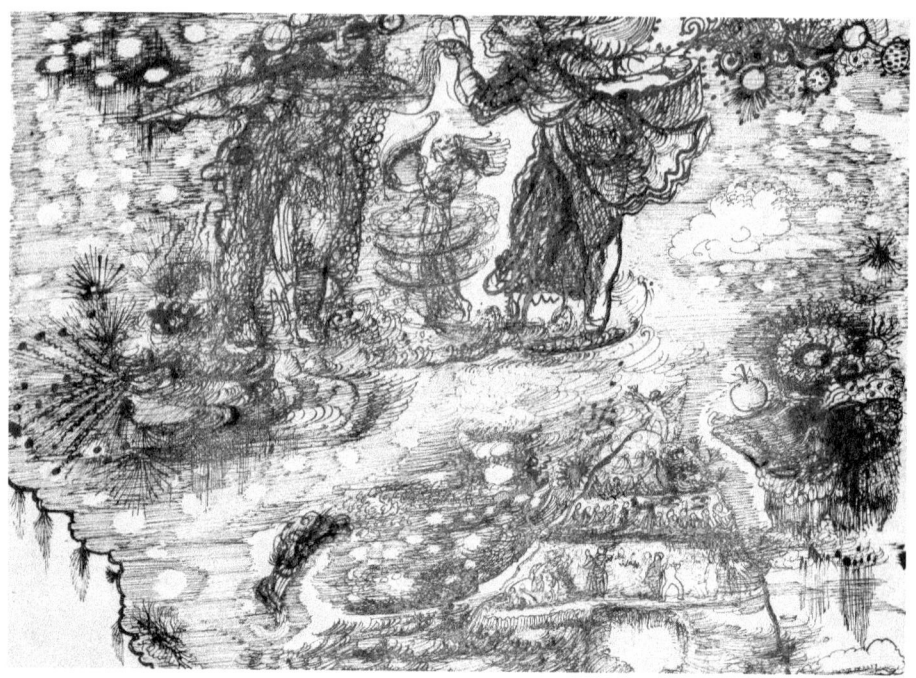

Two costumed women dance or fight in the sky. In between them a small figure swirls. Beneath, a wild sea crashes the shores of 'A Tower of Babylon' where people circle up to a standing figure with arms outstretched. An apple circles in the dark sky around the Tower.

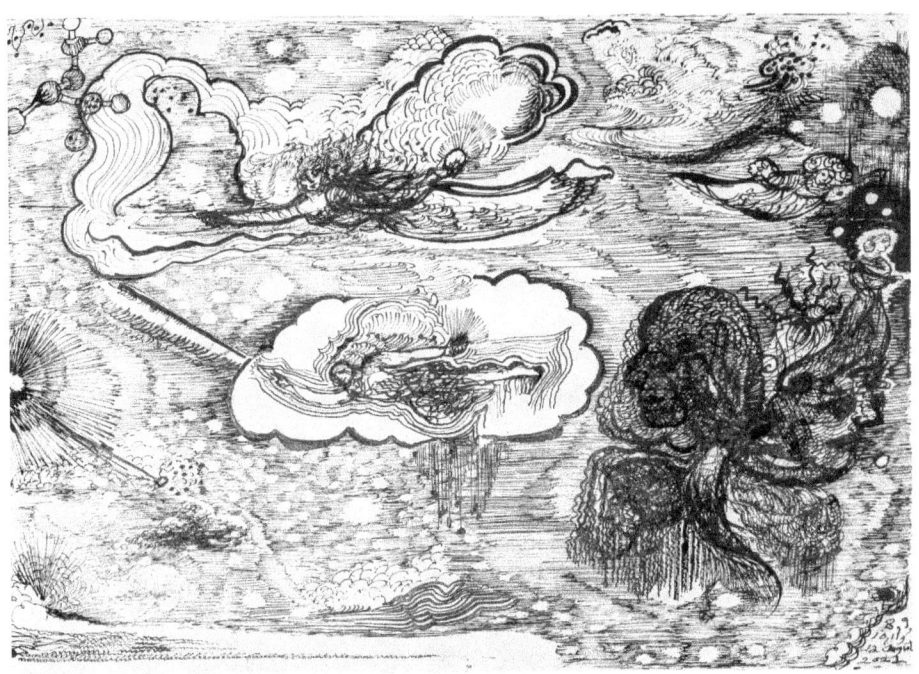

Ambiguous human forms inside two ambiguous clouds in a steady sky. In one corner, a small Molecular Model, near the opposite corner a small flying person. A dark conglomeration of lines form human heads, resembling a butterfly. Someone walks, escapes.

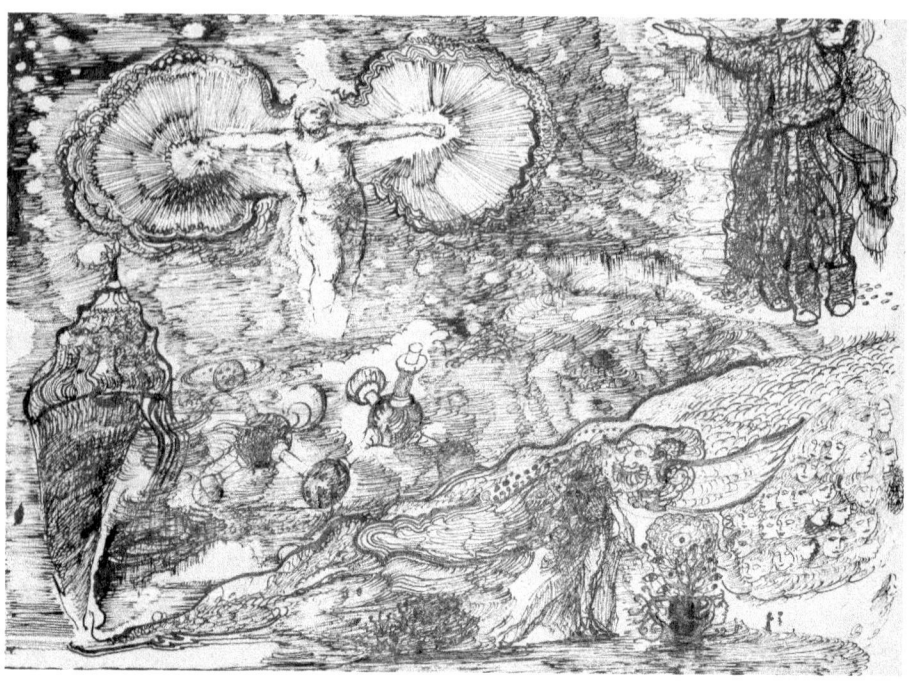

High in the sky, a Christ-like figure's outstretched arms hold large round wings. Opposite, profiles watch a hand. Beneath is a shell, & a Molecular Model. Under a line three small figures are as one, & lower down is a black Medusa before some faint faces.

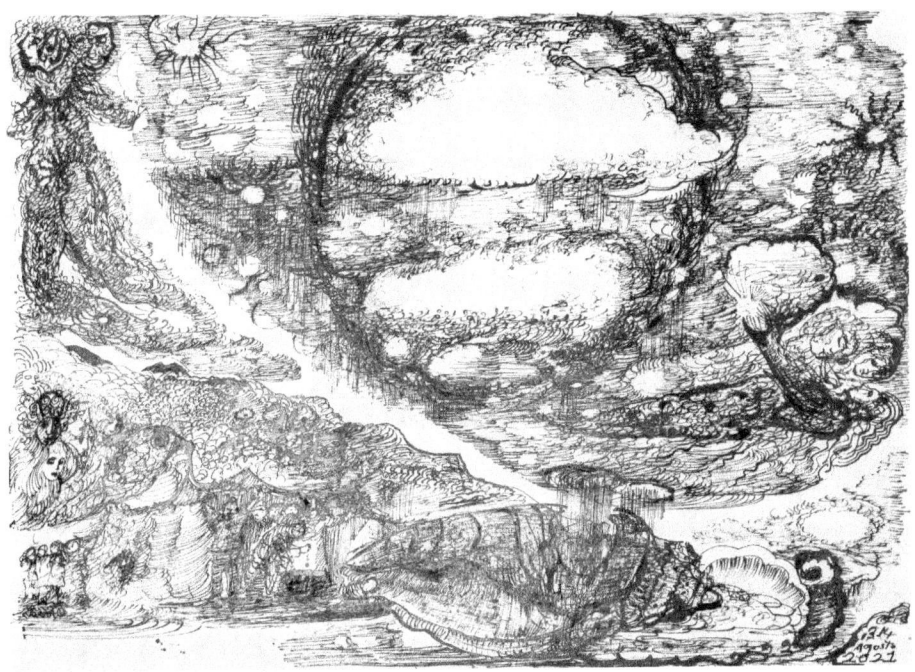

A hybrid human hangs near a white space crossing the page. Clouds float in & out of a large planet whilst three humans as one glide out of the picture. Rock forms merge with the sky, & below people are staring at an enormous shell on its side.

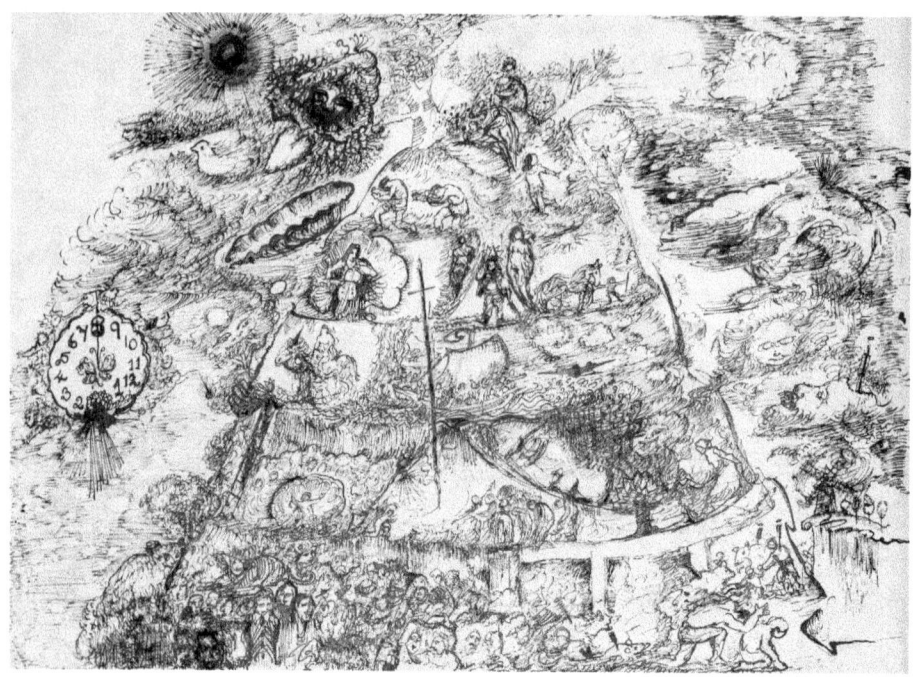

Full page of the 'Tower of Babel'. Women, men, children, animals, a ship, a profile, a shell, a musician, a plane, circle to the human & dog at the top. A clock, a shell, a black hole sun, a bird & a windmill all swirl around.

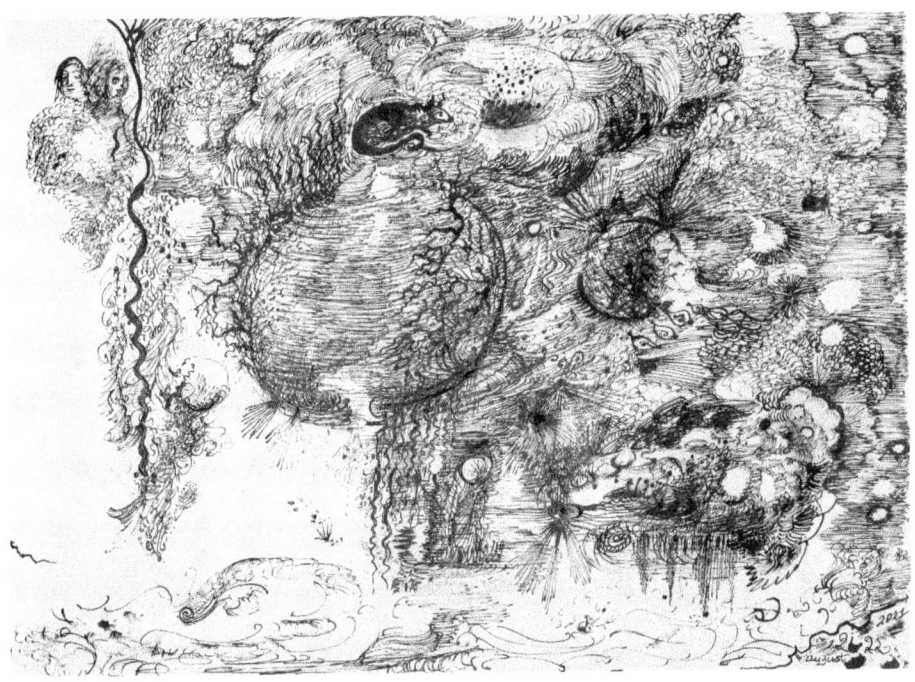

Two small profiles, a rat atop a planet in an abstracted space of scribbles, marks, doodles, lines searching for purpose.

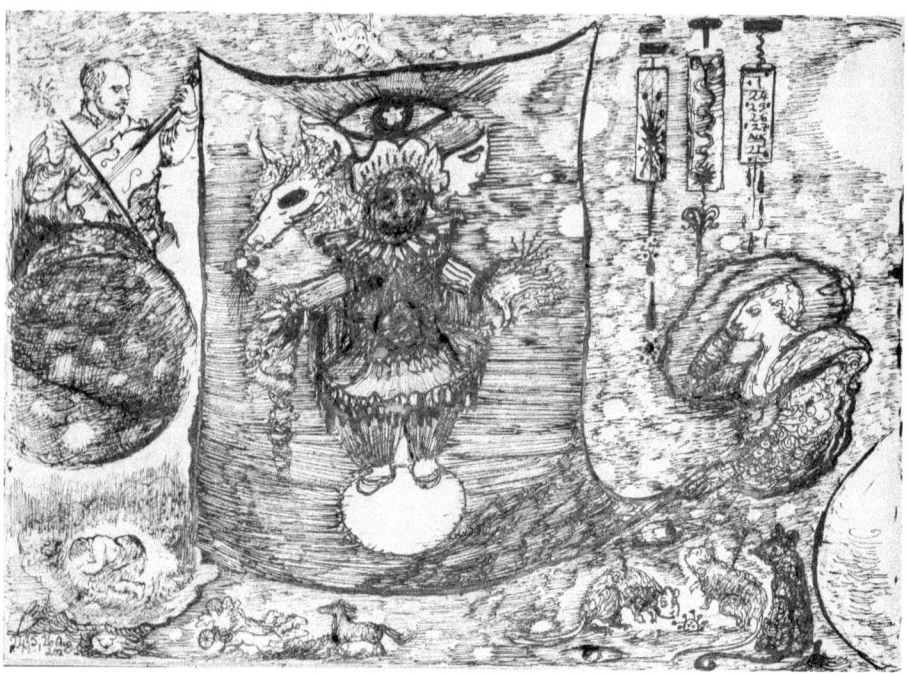

In a page within a page a sad clown stands on a sphere. Behind is a horse's head, a profile & a dark eye. In the margin, Veronese's musician, opposite, the dreaming woman & above her, three toy syringes. Down below, a child sleeps, a wild horse charges at a tiny chariot, & rats converse.

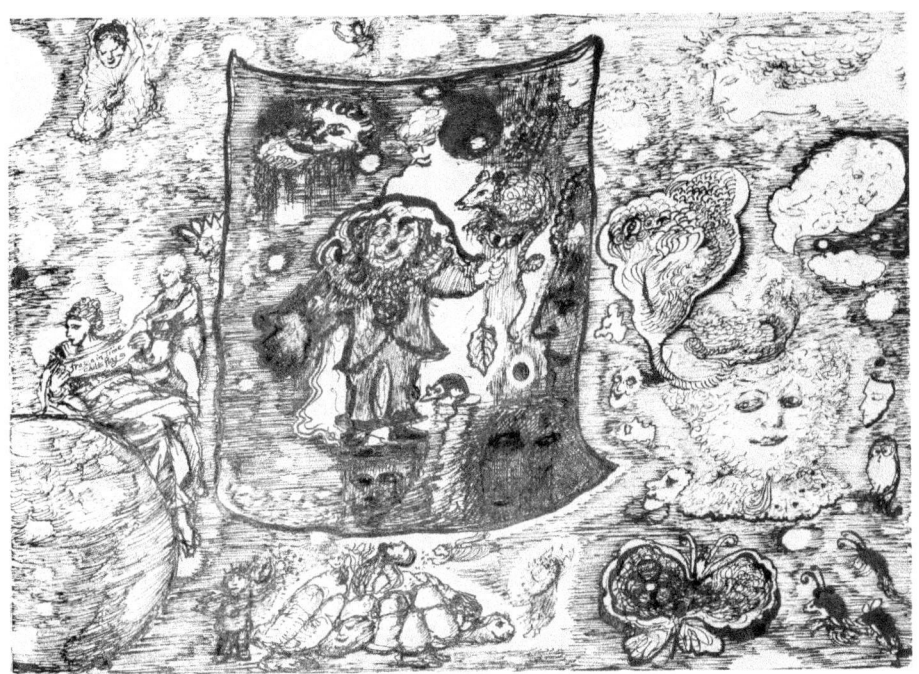

Second page within a page. A clown on a head, a rat at his ankle, holds another, eyes & a leaf. The other hand is gloved. A bearded man grins. In the margin is a butterfly, a dreaming woman & one with a fan. A man bursts from a tortoise. Straddling both pages, sitting atop a large globe, a woman & child hold a banner - 'frozen in time, child's play'.

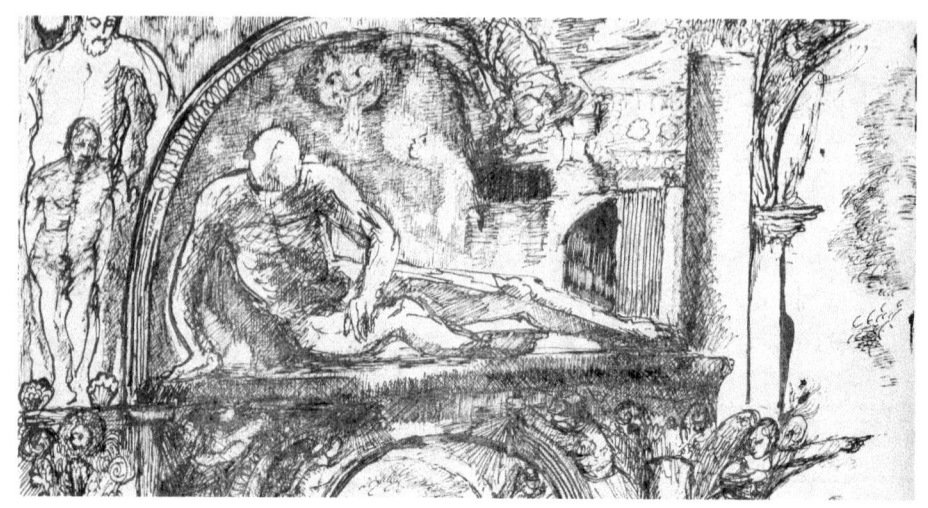

CHAPTER 2
DANCE,CHANCE,TRANCE

What is this book about?
Its certainly not about rats, although they are on pages,
19,20,21,23,24 & 40. I mention them because they can be triggering.
Many featured in the 'The Year 2020 ~ World in Chaos' where
they were associated with the pandemic because of their use in
medical science to benefit humans which I linked to the experimental
COVID-19 vaccine. I wasn't consciously thinking about the pandemic
here - but I'm sure at times, many do, with memories & thoughts
lurking just below the surface.

I can also understand those who want to 'move on', but not holding
those responsible might not be wise in the long run. Those who get
away with wrongdoing usually repeat it.

More people are becoming aware that much needs to be explained,

& that it's more than likely governments have been deliberately dishonest at times.

I now believe most people in government are there for themselves, not the people. My question now is, - how to be positive, knowing things aren't quite right?

I'm convinced that without freedom the imagination suffers, it needs freedom, to think, feel, speculate, question, visualise, daydream, - because it's the contents of these which become the substance of art & science. And for these to materialise, become real, in time & space, a relatively free society is necessary. But at present, laws, rules, regulation, censorship & surveillance are actually increasing.

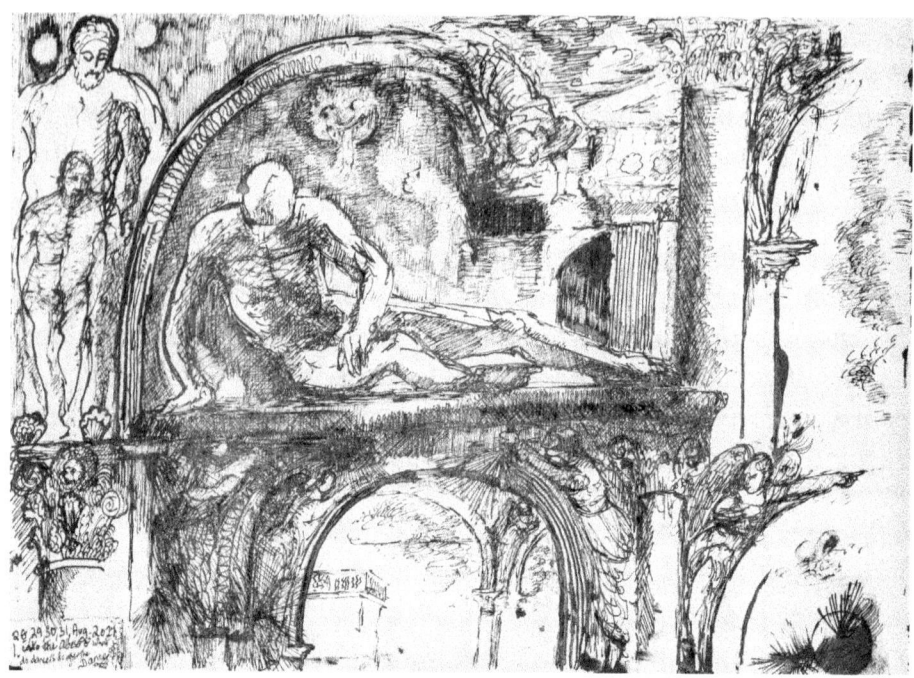

The man peering over a ledge is an 18th Century smuggler. His hung corpse was flayed, then posed & named Smugglerius to mimic the Roman statue of the Dying Gaul, by William Hunter, first RA Anatomy Professor. A falling angel arches over him. A face with a grotesque tongue gloats behind. Also present, a large & small man, temple pediments, arches opening onto others, columns, a balcony, & winged angels.

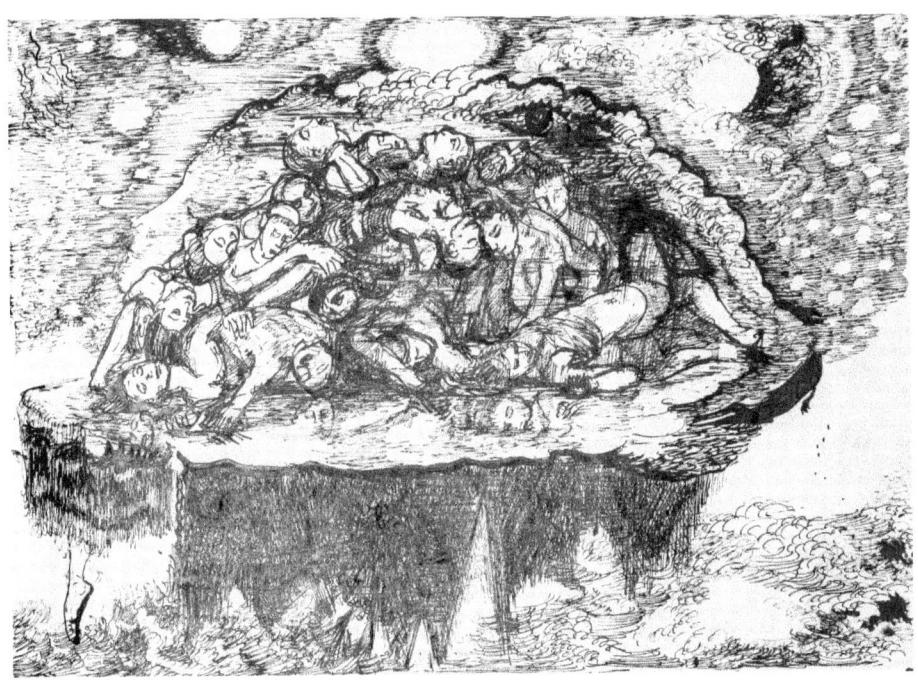

About twenty young people lie heaped on an island edged by a fraying tablecloth hiding eyes & a ballet shoe. Is it drugs, alcohol, exhaustion? They come from 'Flocks', Nir Arieli's dance company. Calm waves lap below.

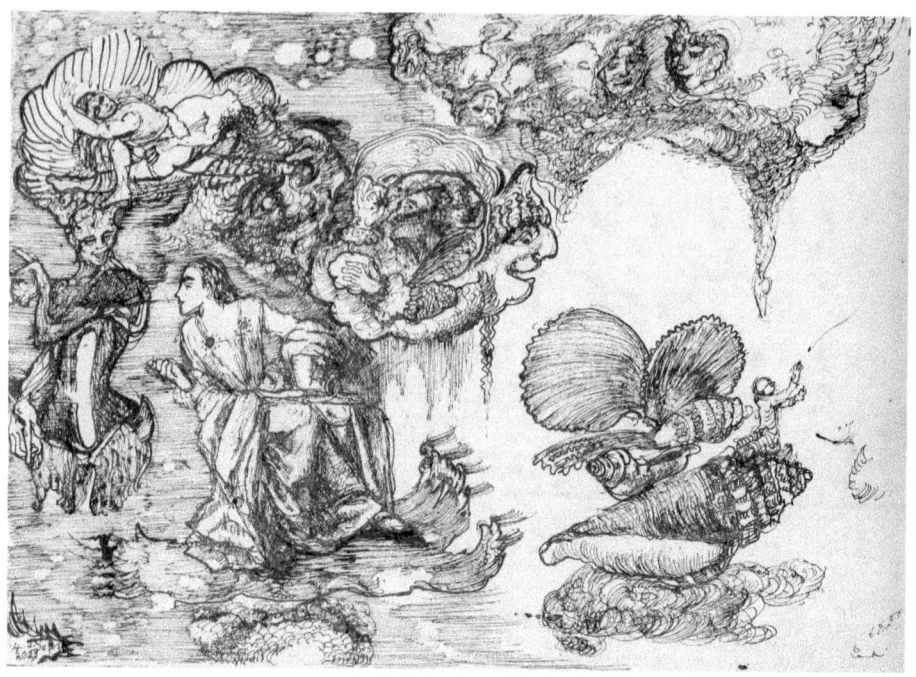

The young woman, from 'The Secret Letter' 1750 by Gaspare Traversi - the Hogarth of Italy, turns to converse with a contemporary half dissected torso - created by Gunther von Hagens. The Torso's head sprouts two lovers, an old lady, & grinning heads. Below, on flying shells with scallops wings, stands a child reaching out.

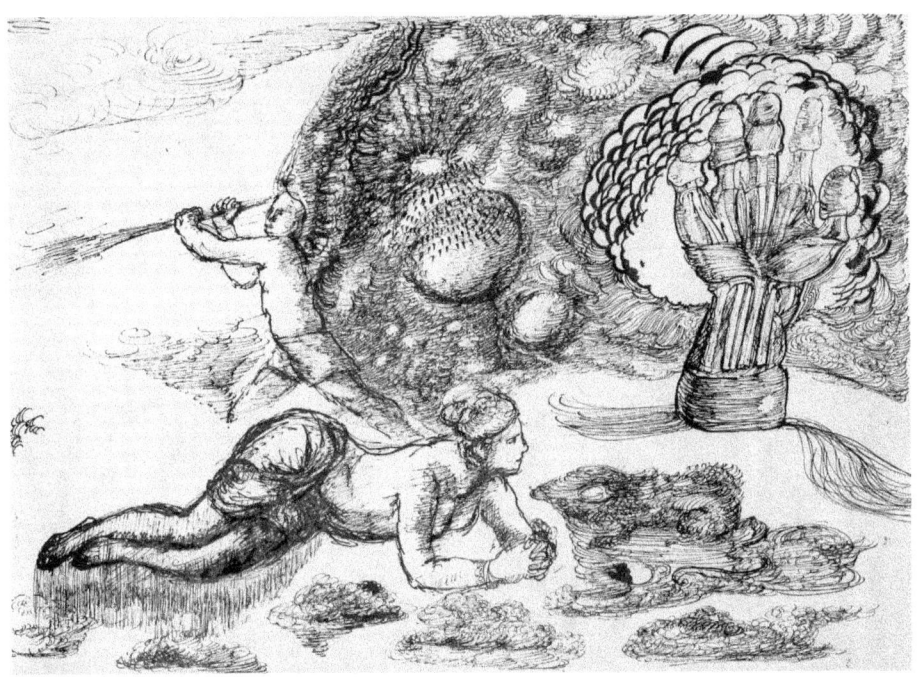

Hovering mid air a woman, with clasped hands looks forward. Behind her is a winged youth. Both are from Cagnacci's painting 'Repentant Magdalene', circa 1660. Above her in a space within space, a hand is outlined.

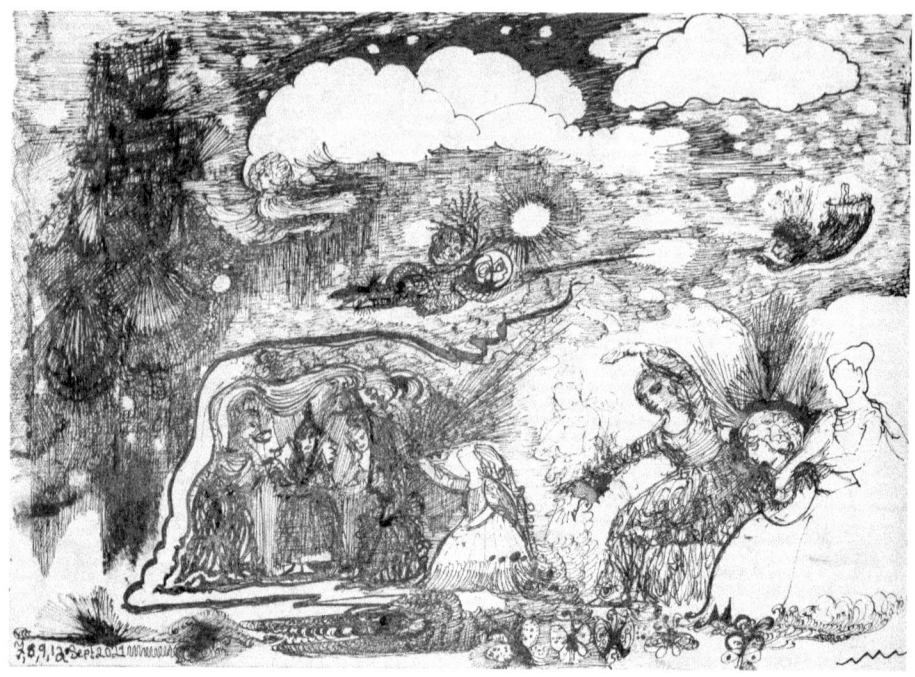

An odd top hatted figure in a dark sky oversees clouds, obscure flying figures, & below, people, & a dancers group in probable lament. Lower still are butterflies & a crocodile head.

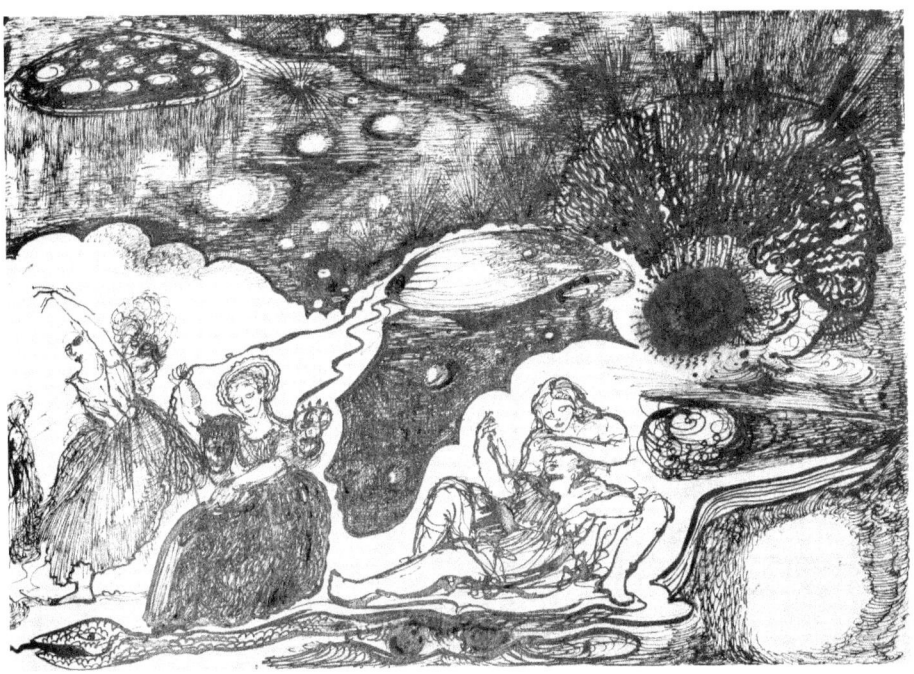

A flat spaceship in a sky with light holes. Beside a profile the sun is extremely dark. Below, two figures, one in black holds a line to the sky & its strange forms. Beside her a girl tends the face of a young man lying on the ground. Below, a blank space, eyes, & a snake.

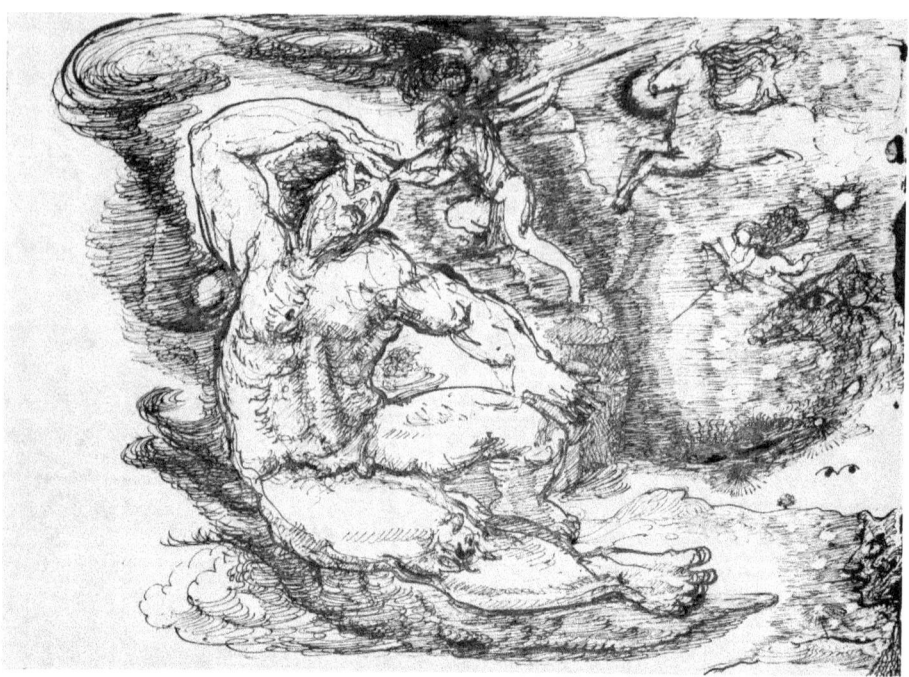

Filing this page is the giant cyclops Polyphemus being blinded by the Questing Ulysses. Around him the sky swirls with a puppet on a horse, & cupid firing at the giant's hand.

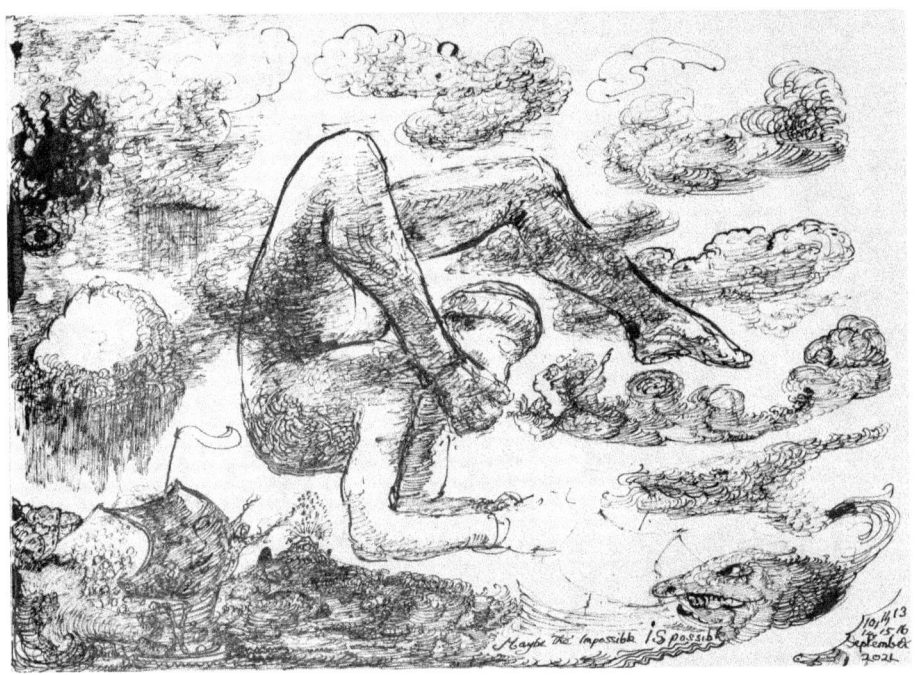

Clouds float in & out of an acrobat whose leg is bent so far over his head, it hides one eye. The closed one blinds him to an apparition flying at him. Floating near is a jellyfish, a Ship of Fools, a face on its mainsail, a volcano, an empty ship & a fierce fish. Words say - 'Maybe the impossible is possible'.

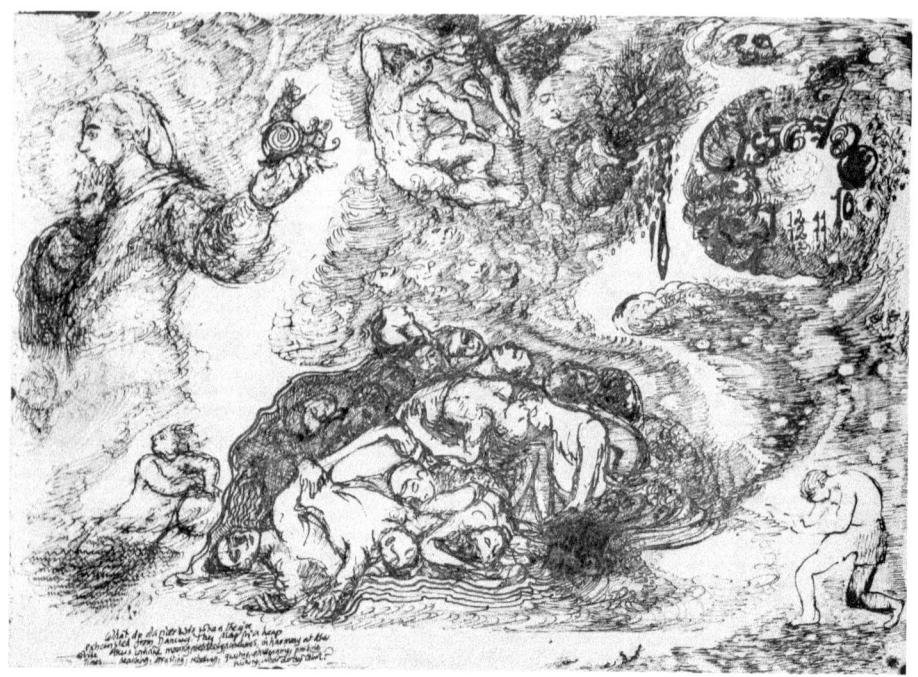

The heaped dancers have not woken. Above written lines, the dreaming man rises from the sea clutching a ball. The large woman shields her face with one hand, the other holds a snail sees the scene. High up, Cyclops is blinded again. A moon, circle of numbers, & a man, head down, fists clenched enters from the left.

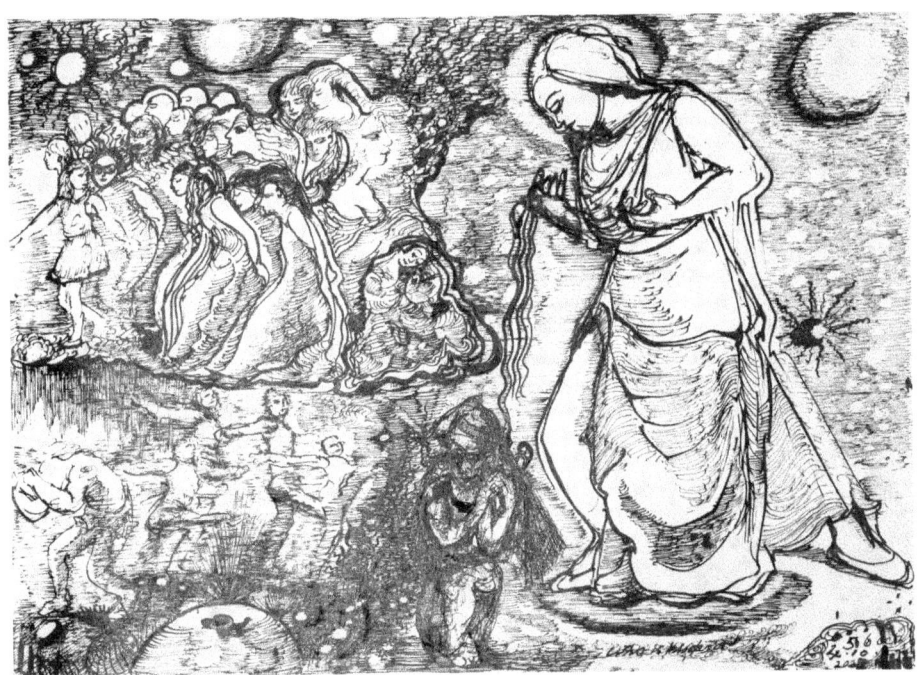

Nina Yerchinina, dancer in the 1933 ballet 'Choreartium' based on Brahms 4th, stands in the sky. Her head lowered, hands gesturing intensely, women & girls march away from her, but others look back. Below, a planet spins, young men from Crystal Pites dance 'Flight Pattern' march towards Nina. In the forefront a dark Aphrodite crouches.

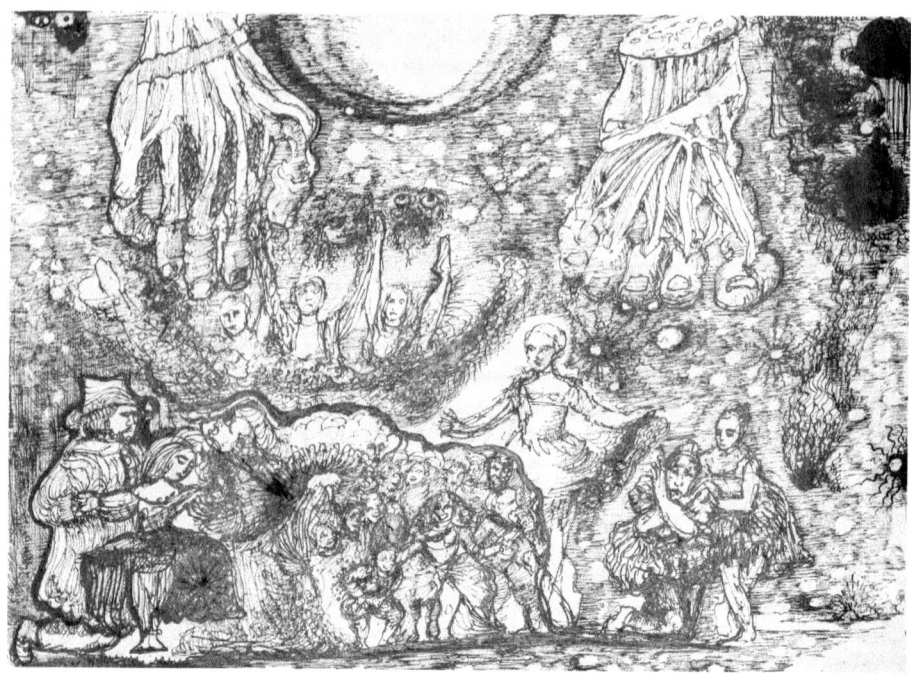

A planet hangs between a half dissected hand, a foot, & a large profile. Three young people raise their arms. A ballet dancer watches over a performance of Handel's 'Soul' at Glyndenbourne. A ballerina comforts a crouching clown.

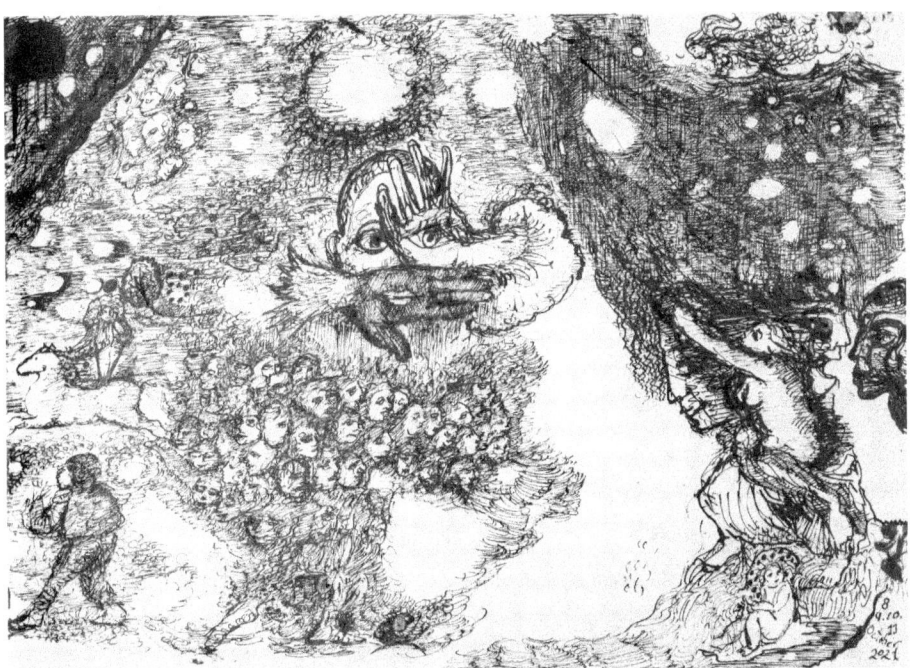

Sketchily drawn legs support many heads looking this way & that. Above, a large face has an eye in one palm, lips in the other, from Opera Factory's 'Satyricon'. A woman opens a curtain with holes & profiles. Near her is a child. Opposite a clown stands on a horse & someone walks away.

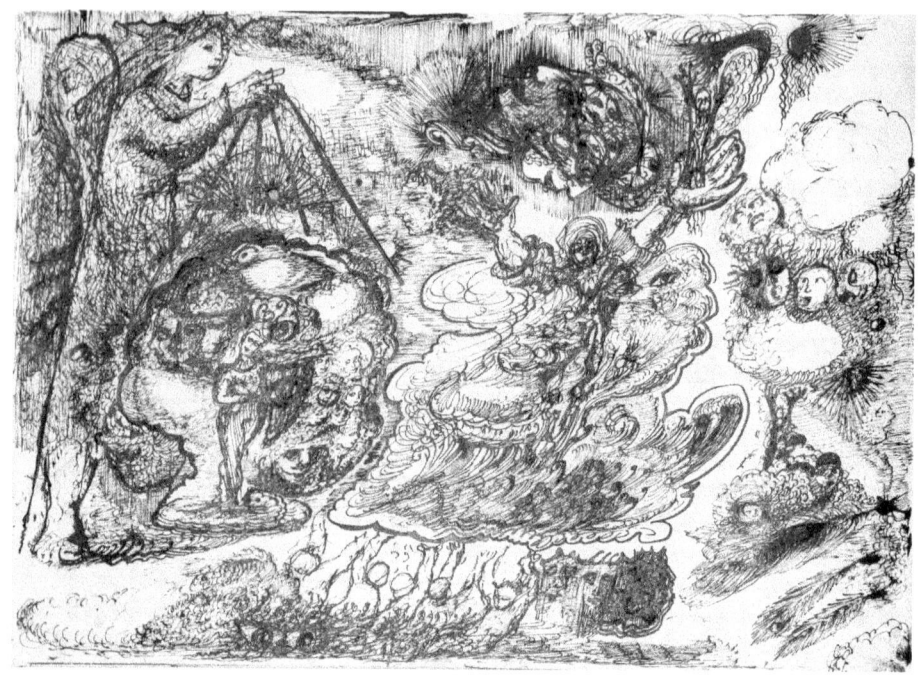

A tall winged being holds a sextant over outlined heads, & a clown. In the centre someone with huge hands reaches up to a staring profile & dark heads while underneath, others reach up from waves. Three faces hang. Figures spiral into clouds.

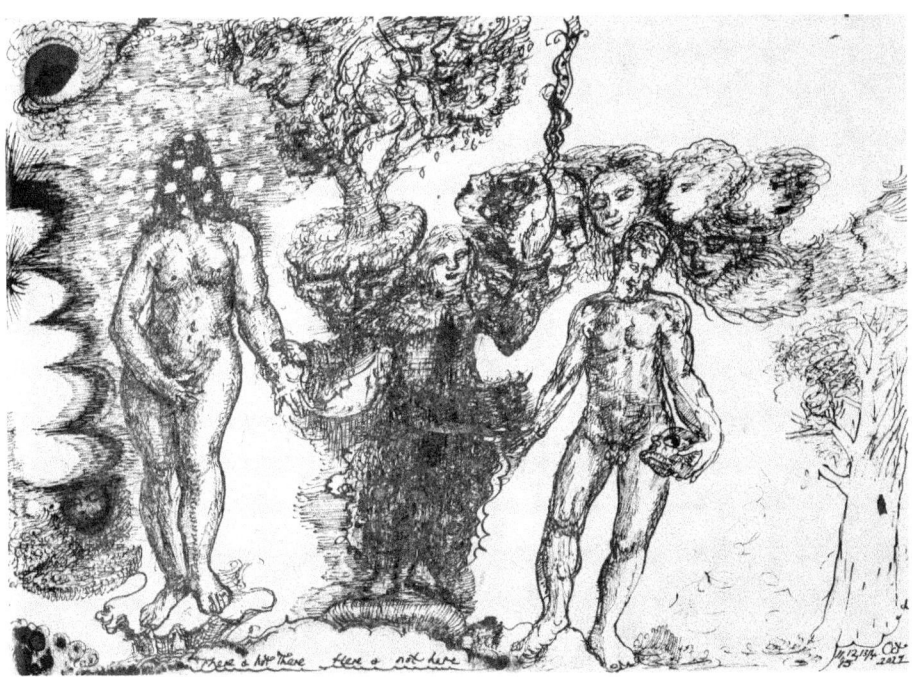

A naked man & woman face the viewer. Behind her is a holy sky & over her head is a scarf with holes, he holds a skull. Both hold the hand of the woman between them whose skirt is made of faces. From her right shoulder faces sprout, & from them, others & then a tree. On her other shoulder seven faces commune.

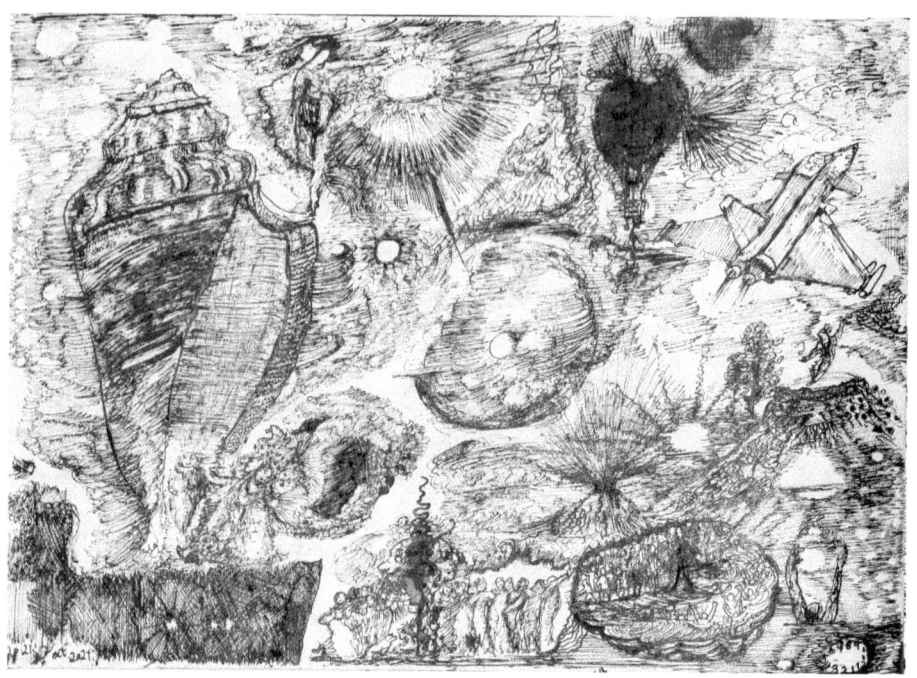

At the base of a giant shell people enter or leave. A jet soars, someone leaps from one of two volcanoes. There are trees, a black sun, a black air ballon, planets spin, people drown, others process.

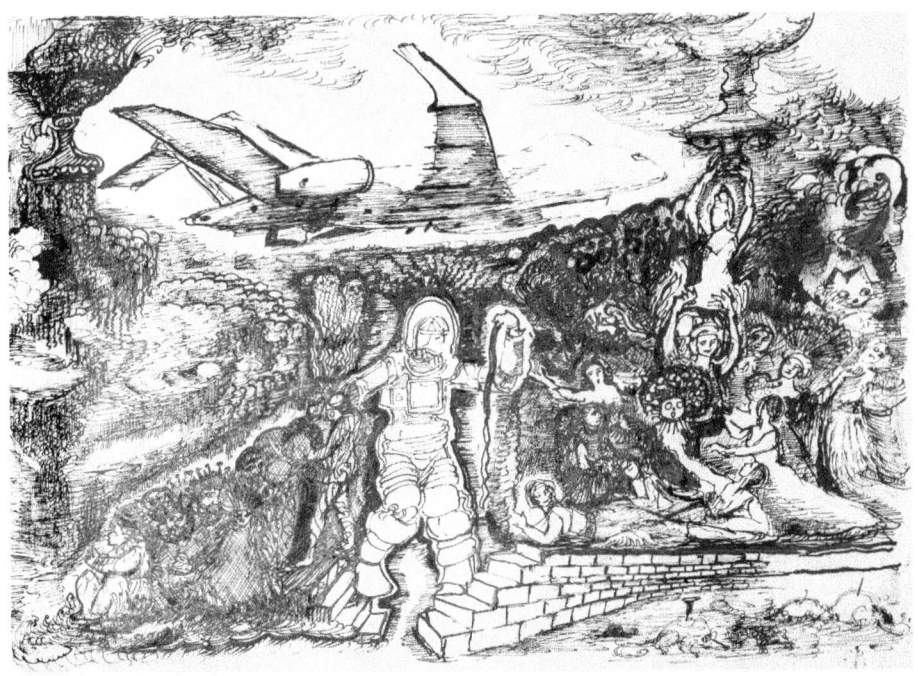

A large jet roars over an astronaut in hazmat gear. He has divided a group of people by bursting through a wall where rats swim. On his left a dancer raises a chalice, on his right, owls stare over people huddled together, dark mist spirals up from them to a black chalice.

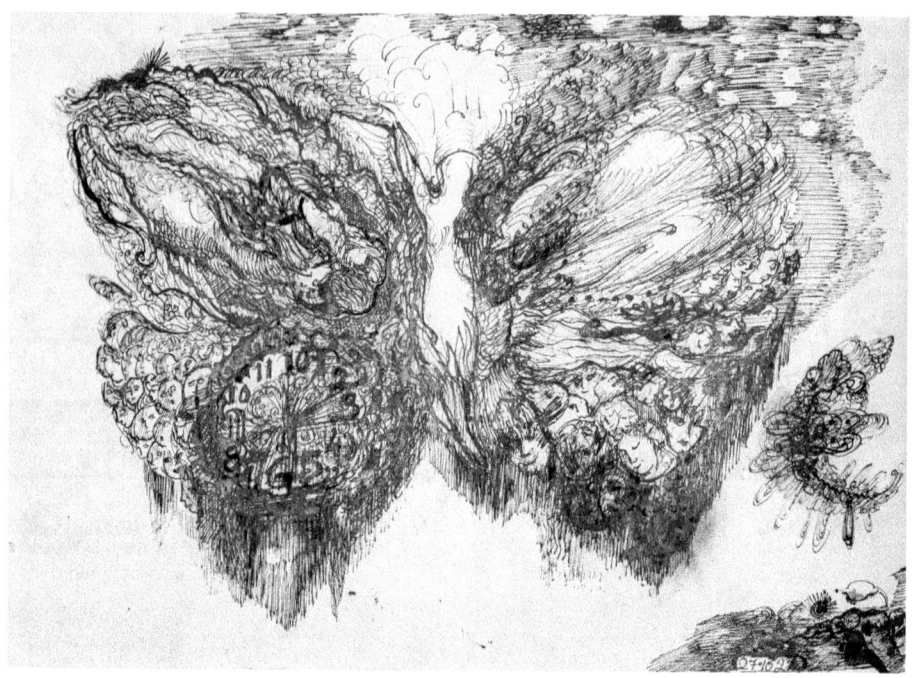

In the centre hovers a butterfly with the body of a faceless human, with upper wings of abstracted lines. In the lower wings are faces & a clock with anti-clockwise numbers.

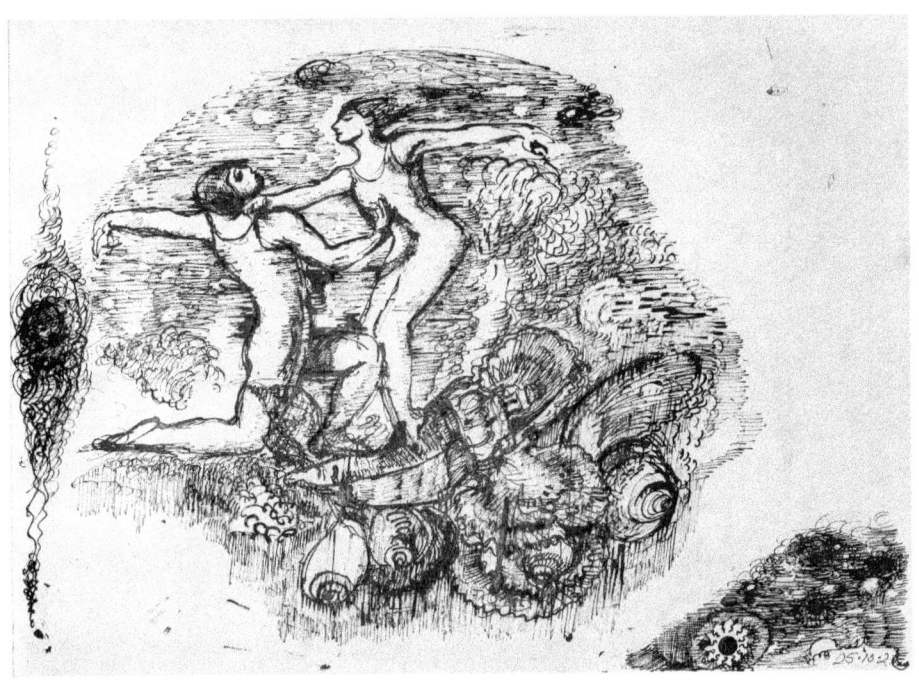

In a scratchy patchy sky a pair of dancers are poised together atop a cluster of seashells. Doodles can be seen in the margins either side.

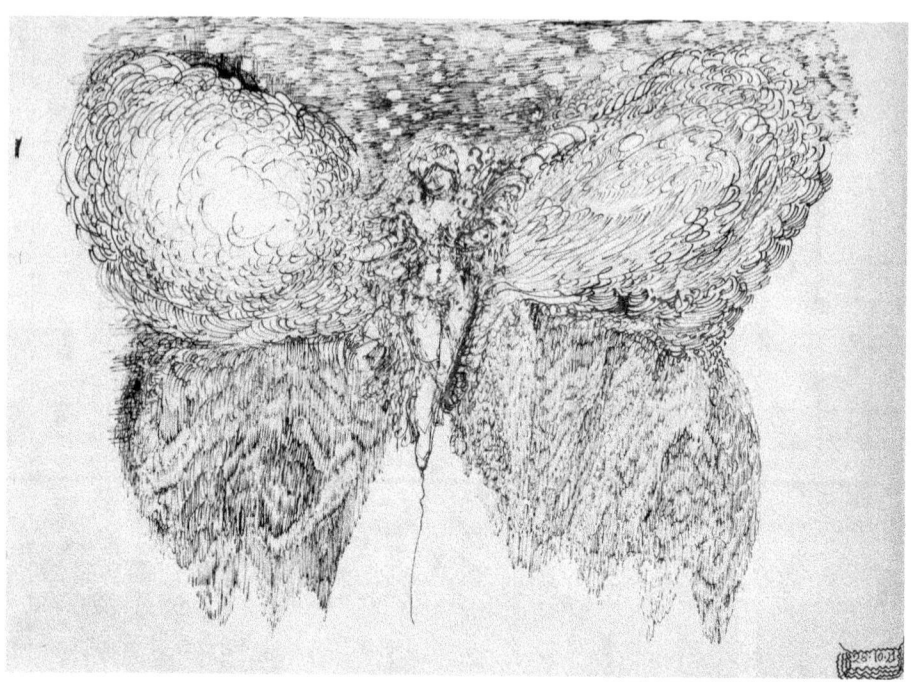

Beneath a sky pierced with stars a solitary butterfly with unadorned wings hangs in space, home to a human with a thoughtful expression.

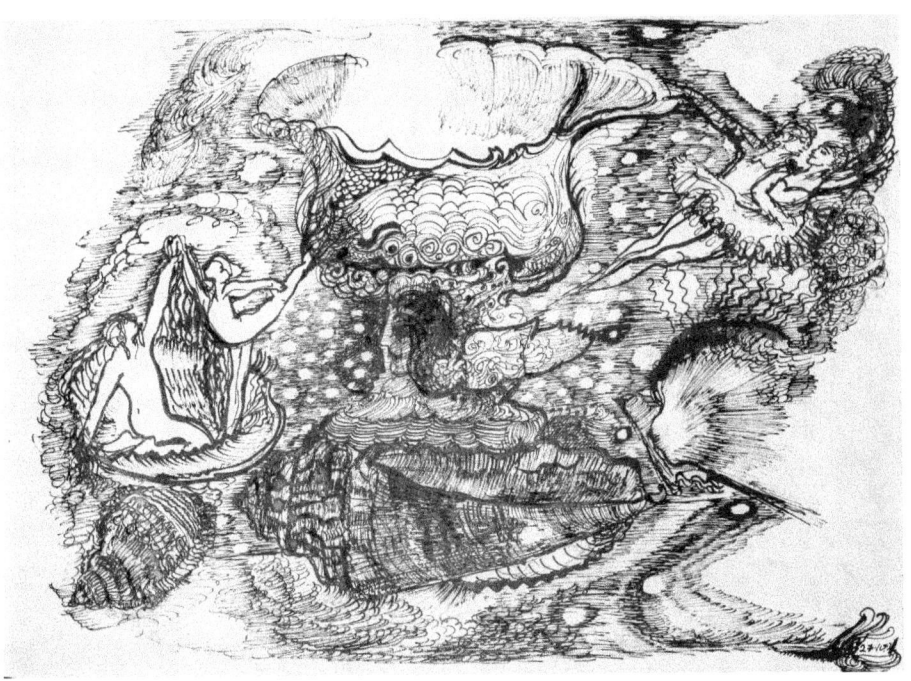

In the centre a stylised chalice has a profile resting on top of a giant shell. Either side are ballet dancers, the left pair dance in a scallop shell, those on the right float out into space.

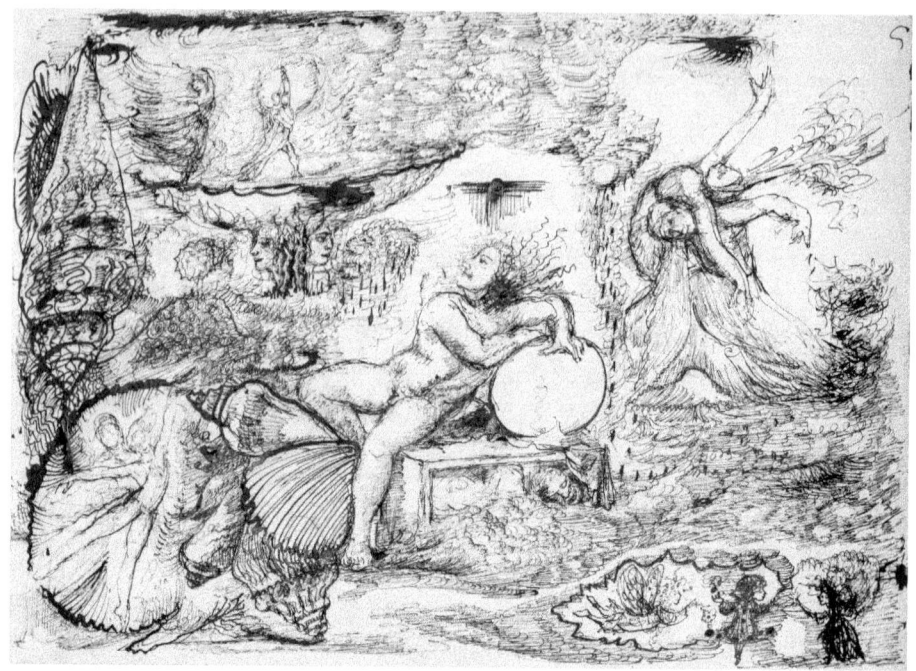

From Michelangelo's workshop comes the 'Dream of Human Life' with his globe, presiding over pairs of swirling dancers, shells, profiles, a volcano, clouds. Fairies converse far below.

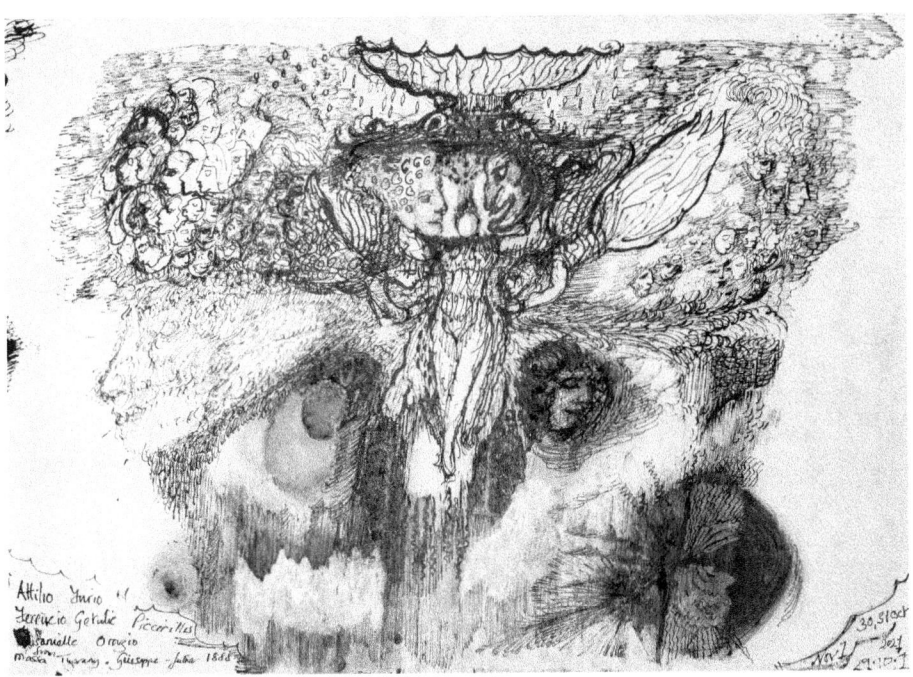

A man & woman wear Pantomime masks, are hatted by a chalice
& share a body. Wing shapes flank them & below lie, three profiles
with a black planet. Writing in left corner, the Piccirilli, were six
Italian brothers famous for sculpting & carving all over America.

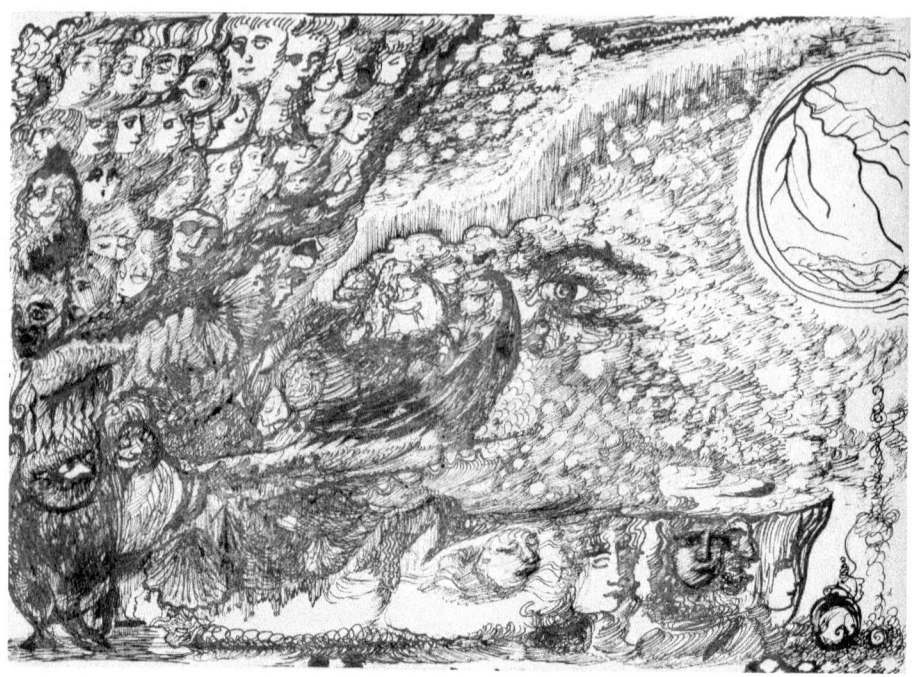

Densely packed faces of a planet or curtain merges into the sky. Below indecipherable characters & a fish stares at a human & dog aboard a ship. An eye hovers. Profiles process below. Above a lined circle leaves.

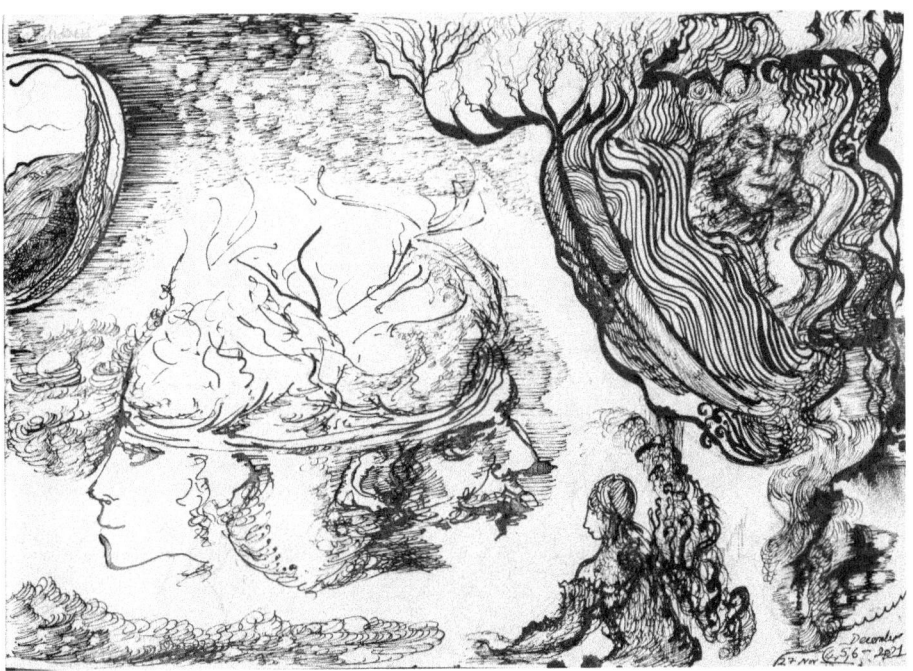

Random lines burst from a hollow skull. Either side of which are bold profiles of a man & woman. To one side a stylised curtain sprouts twigs & contains a sad face. A young woman in the foreground looks on.

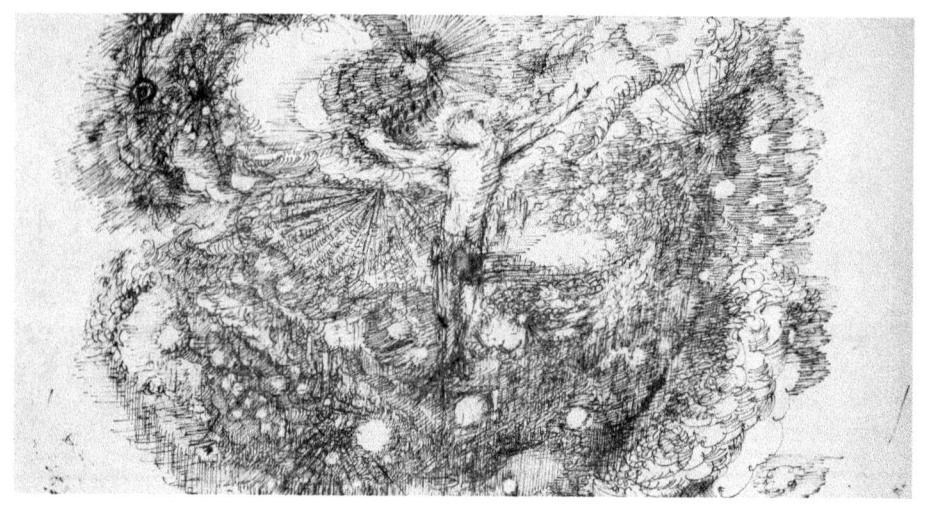

CHAPTER 3 ENANTIODROMIA

Enantiodromia, meaning - things turning into their opposites.

Concluding thoughts on the drawings.
Although almost done, the book had no narrative, only questions - what is truly important in life - relationships, love, community, security, freedom, meaning beyond the material world or technology?

And why so many butterflies? Starting as eggs, then forming a chrysalis & finally a butterfly, they're seen as symbols of transformation. And because of their fragility they're also associated with the soul, spirit, Gnosticism & Christianity.

Two particular books have influenced this one. First, Andreas Vesalius's 1543 book of etchings of the human body, from the skeleton to the skin. Because of that early research & discovery most people have some knowledge of how our bodies work. Is an equal understanding of the brain possible?

Dr Iain McGilChrist's 2009 book - 'The Master & His Emissary' has a clue. He researches into the differences & relationship between the right & left hand sides of the brain & plausibly explains how & why our lives today are so affected by computers. They undoubtedly provide extraordinary convenience but can also lead to excessive control & become a real threat to freedom. Put simply the book presents evidence indicating that the left side which controls measurement, logic, science, reason, numbers etc has taken control over the right - of the imagination, ideas, art, poetry, literature, music, painting, etc. This book made me rethink many things about today's world.

Without computers this book wouldn't exist. And I don't want to live without modern dentistry, surgery & more. People of my generation remember life before mobiles & computers which younger ones obviously can't. But never before have so many people been so dependent on a technology, which few have any knowledge of at all. I don't even know how a light bulb works.

It's not possible or desirable to stop science. Many might argue otherwise, but technology has limits, - robots don't have blood & will probably never draw like Leonardo da Vinci or carve like Michelangelo.

And it's not unreasonable to question increasing camera surveillance, the cashless society, data harvesting, phone alert apps, political propaganda, & censorship. Are these the price of convenience or is there a way to have the convenience but not the control?

One way might be to use less tech & the imagination more. It's not limited & its free.

Imagination, that sliver of mental activity just outside of everyday thoughts, worries, fears, emotions, feelings, - hovering at the edge, hoping to be noticed...waiting, wanting to slip into consciousness.

If this book is about anything it's about the imagination. I'm sure *everyone who wants to, can connect with it, develop it, have their own relationship with it. In society the role & place of the imagination can be found in the ideas leading to the creation of the arts & sciences, which weren't thought of as separate until the 17th Century.* What separated them, & where will it lead?Perhaps the subject for another book of drawings.

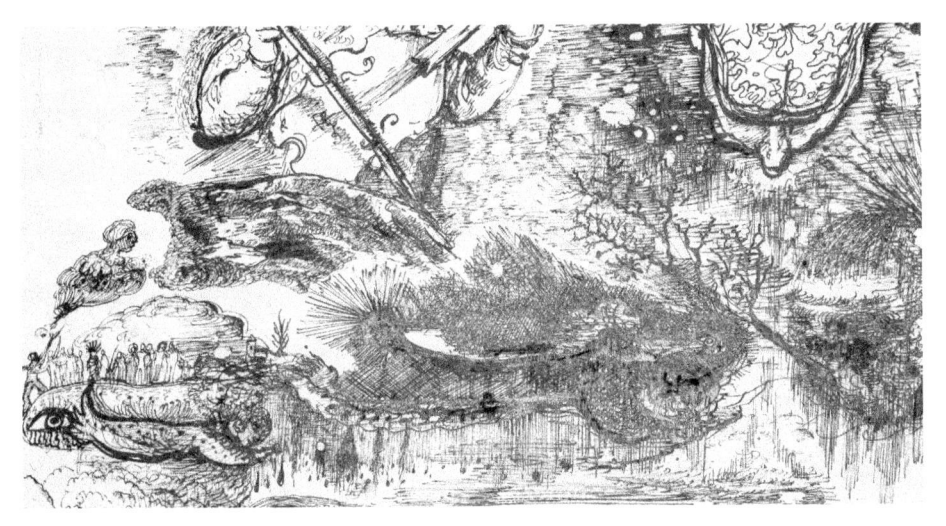

CHAPTER 4

DEEPER DIVE DEEPER

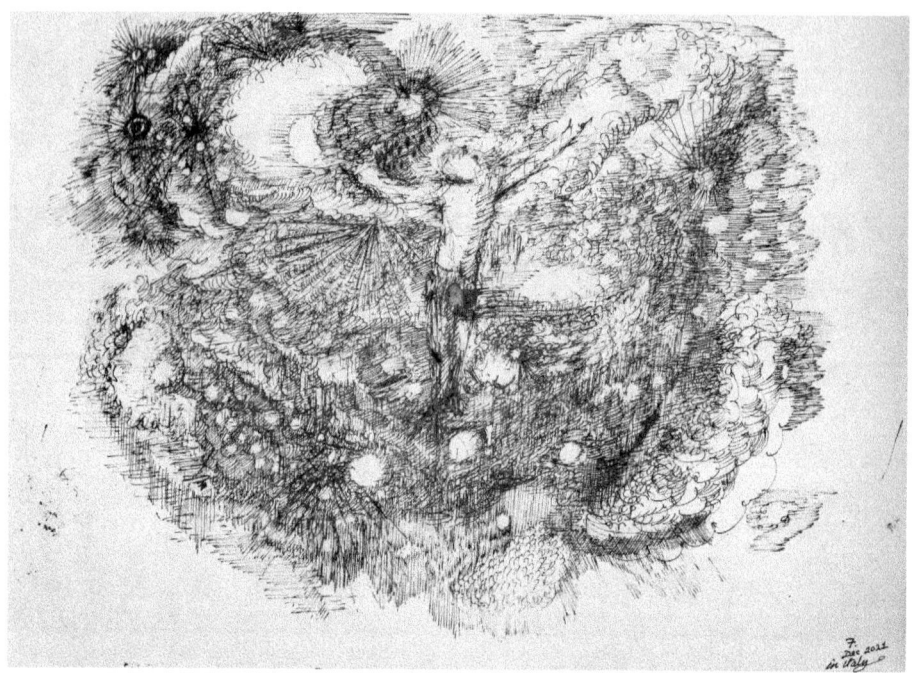

A butterfly? Whatever it is, there is a human at the centre who appears to silently float. The wings as such, depict stars, with rays & bursts of light.

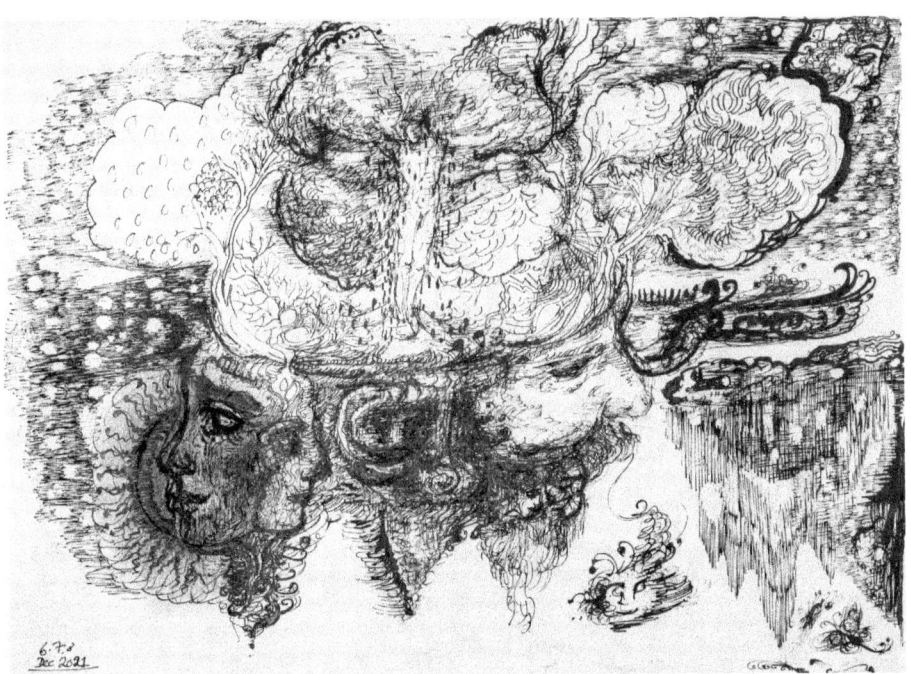

A human's outstretched arms resemble butterflies' wings. Rain falls either side of him & trees have roots growing from the scene below, where two females face away from a male profile, while another looks towards him. He looks away from all three at a conflagration of lines. Other lines between them suggest ears.

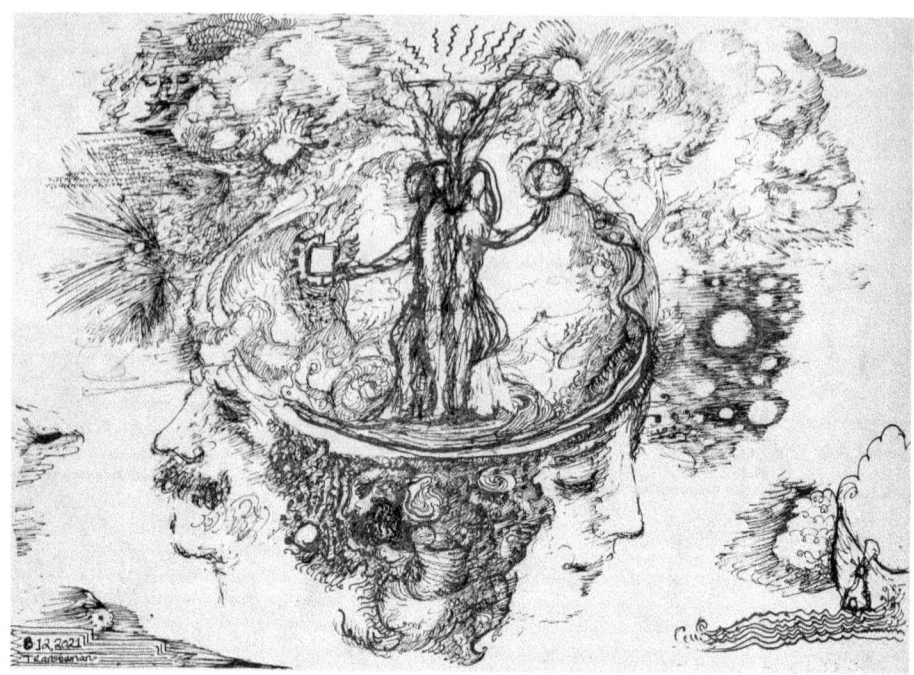

Two figures struggle, separate to finally emerge from the centre of a skull. A triangle issues from their heads into a sky busy with clouds, holes & rays. To the right a woman looks down, & on the left a male looks straight ahead.

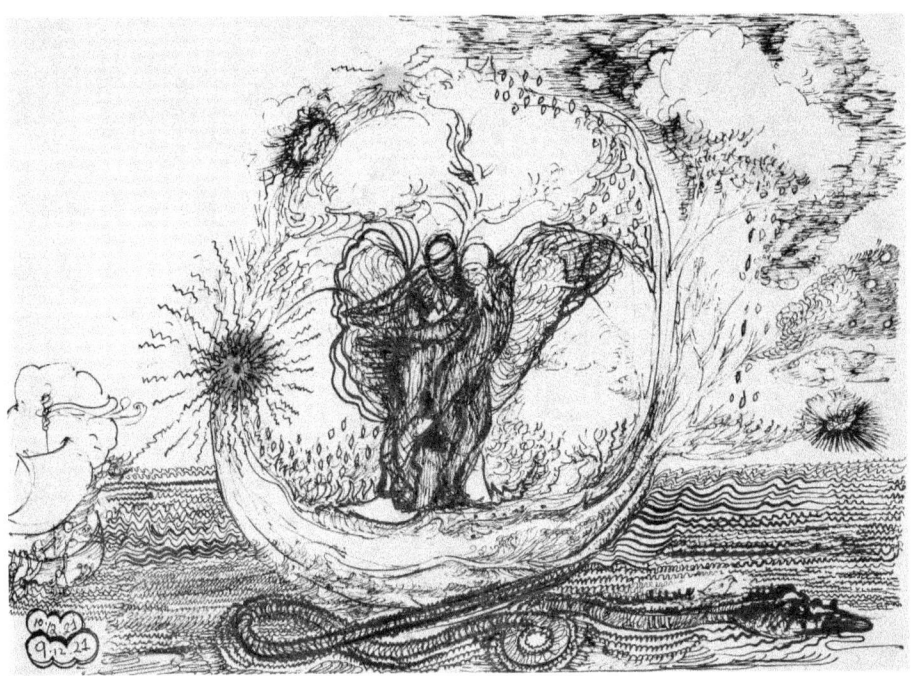

Passengers fall overboard from a 'Ship of Fools' sailing across both pages towards a large ship with a dark sun on the stern, & a tree joining clouds at the prow. Inside, under branches & leaves, a winged couple dance. Lines form a calm ocean. Under the ship lurks a large sea snake.

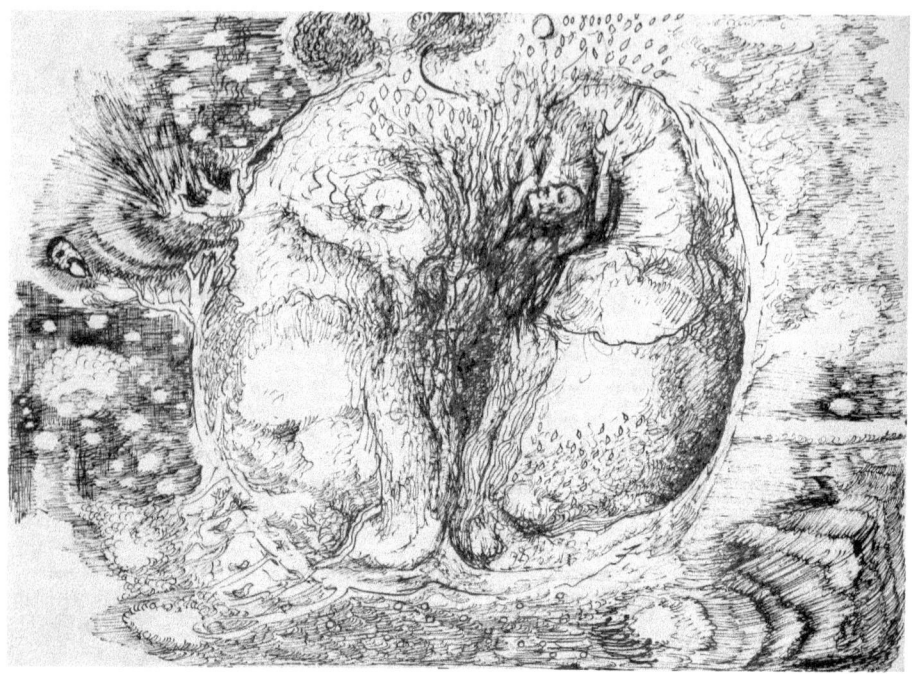

Two interlocked humans with closed eyes, try to escape upwards from the bone layers of a skull. Branches, leaves, & a mottled sky surround the scene.

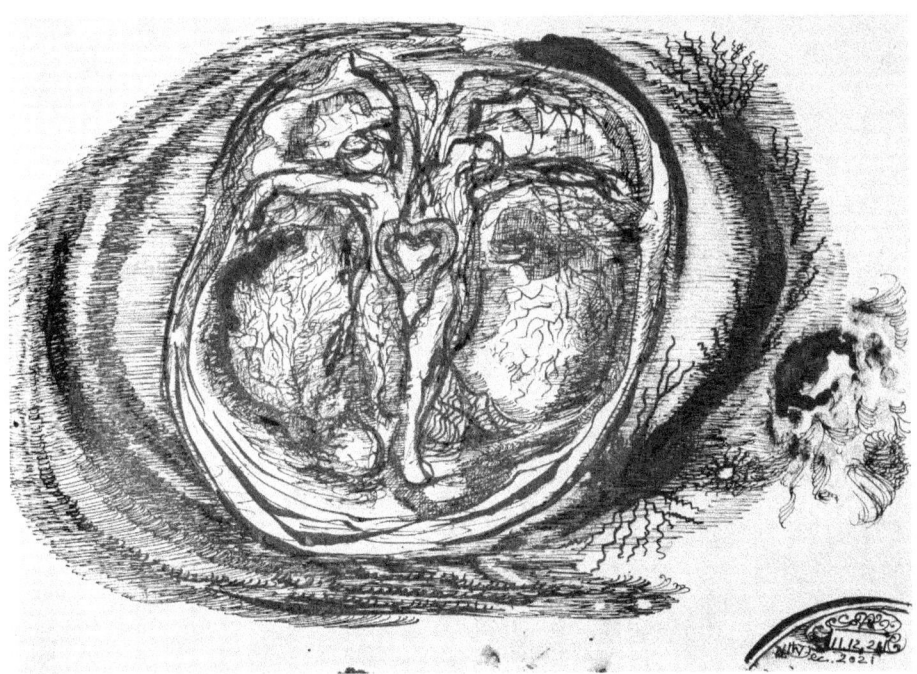

Alternating dark & light concentric lines surround two tentative figures, embracing, arms reaching up & out, a bold heart at their centre.

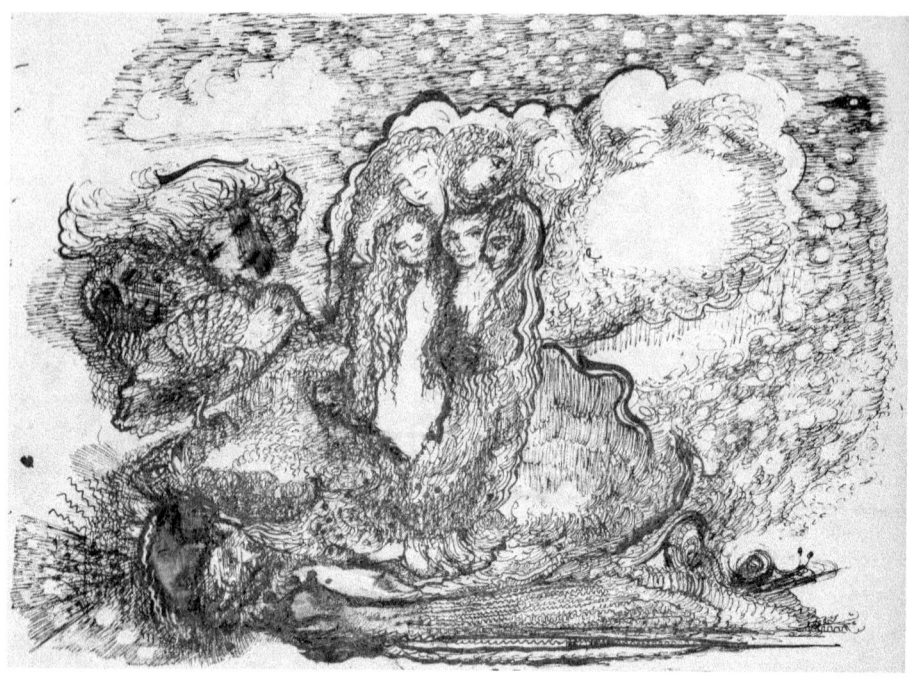

Rocks & shells merge in which five women group together. To their left is a bird & two faces, empty space on their right. Below, rays surround a sad face while opposite a snail slowly moves.

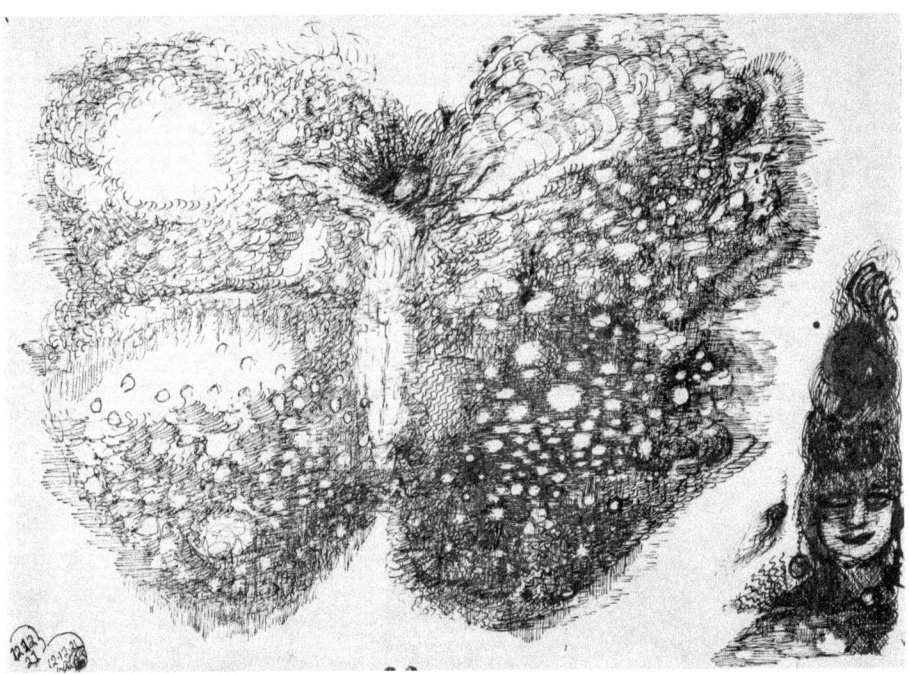

Hovering in empty sky is a human in the centre of a large butterfly. The wings, of points, from right to left form an increasingly dark background. A woman wearing a large black hat stares at us from the edge of the page.

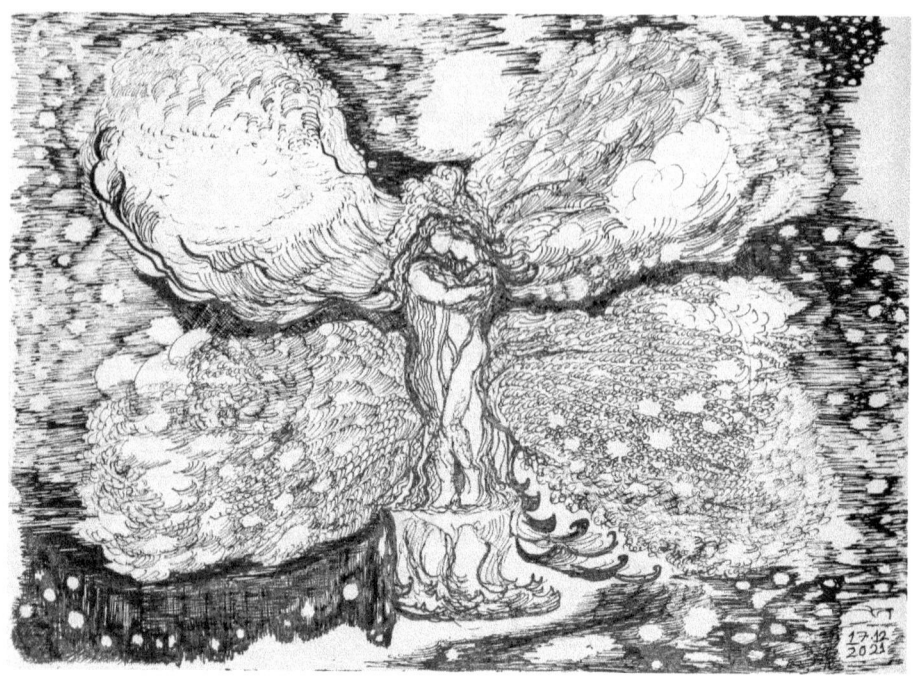

Two figures on a plinth embrace. From their centre, filling the page come four huge wings composed of nothing more than clouds, light holes & stars. Contrasting dark & light is visible just outside this vision.

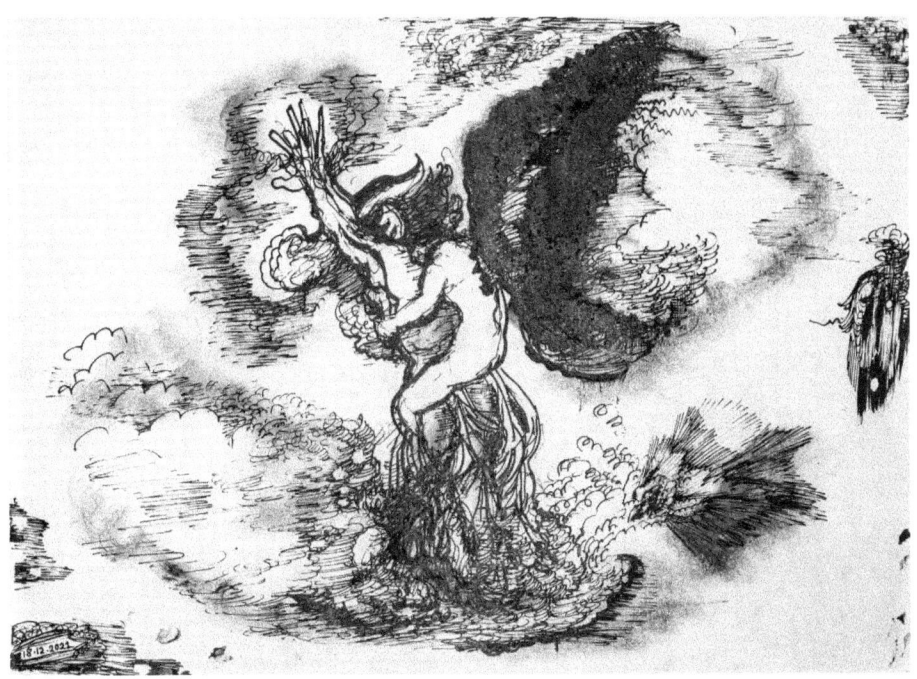

A couple, rising from the sea into the clouds hold each other tightly as they embark on an unknown journey. The enlarged hand of one reaches up, the other clings. Is a wing or shadow attached to them?

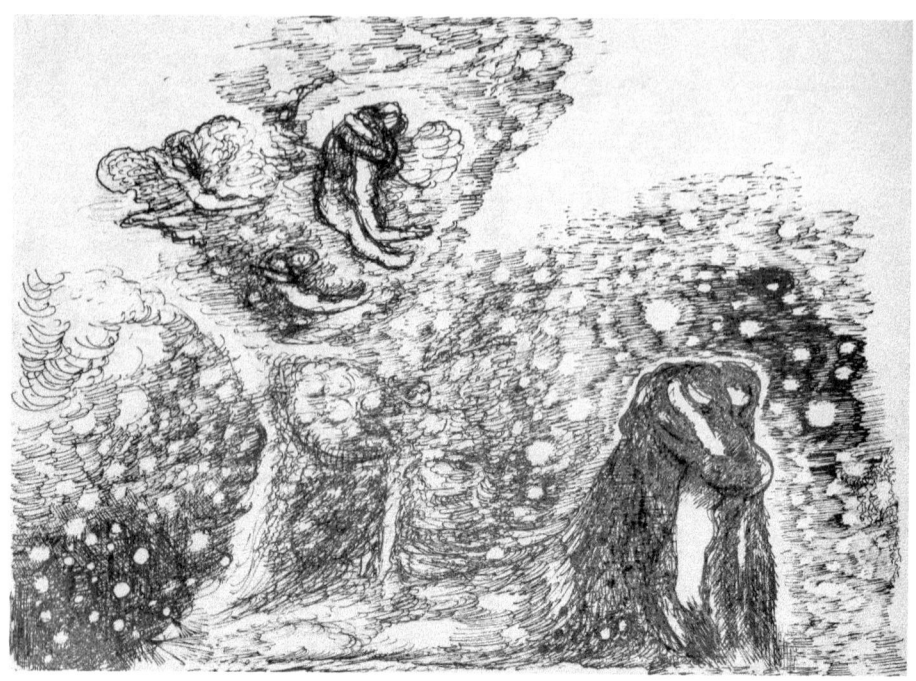

A sky with stars & light holes fills most of the page where several couples passionately embrace, cling in flight or swim in clouds & where a woman in the centre seems to emerge from nowhere.

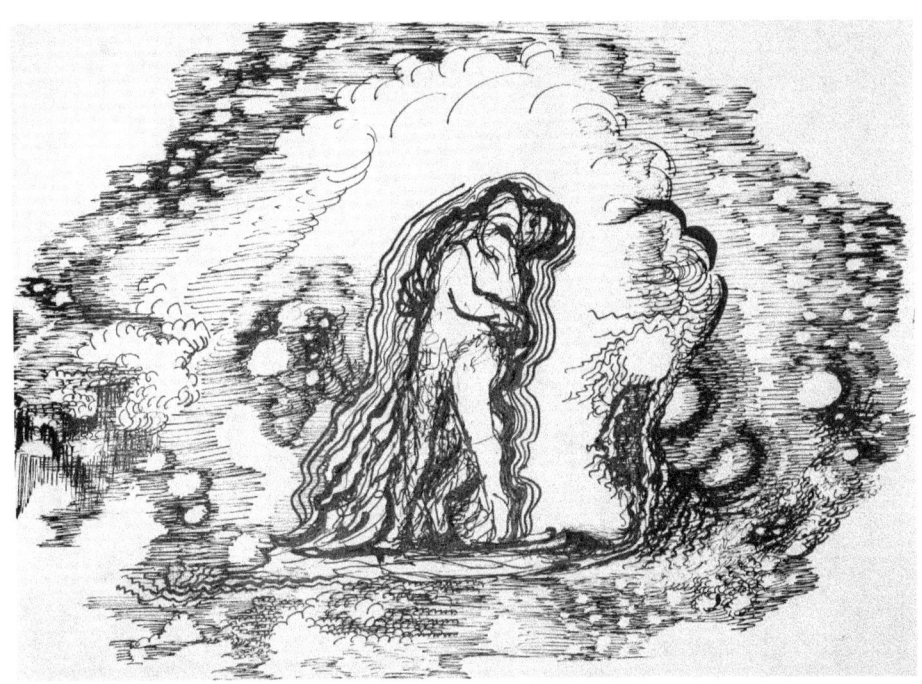

On a cloud, in a sky of stars stands a couple, outlined in several lines, who are entwined, desperate, clinging, fearful of what? A profile is seen at their side.

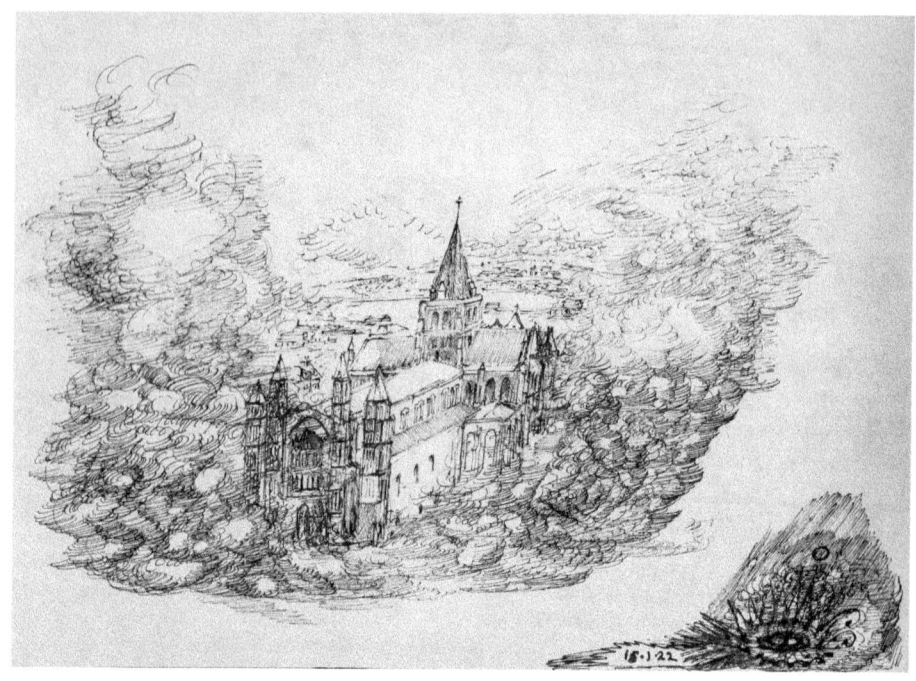

Rochester Cathedral, 604 AD, the second oldest in England, suddenly appears. It's home to the famous Textus Roffensis 1120, two illustrated books in one, of ancient 600 AD English law & codes from King Alfred the Great, Athelstan, Ethelred the Unready, & Cnut, to the lives of women, men, children, the enslaved & free, the rich & the poor. Online & in the crypt.

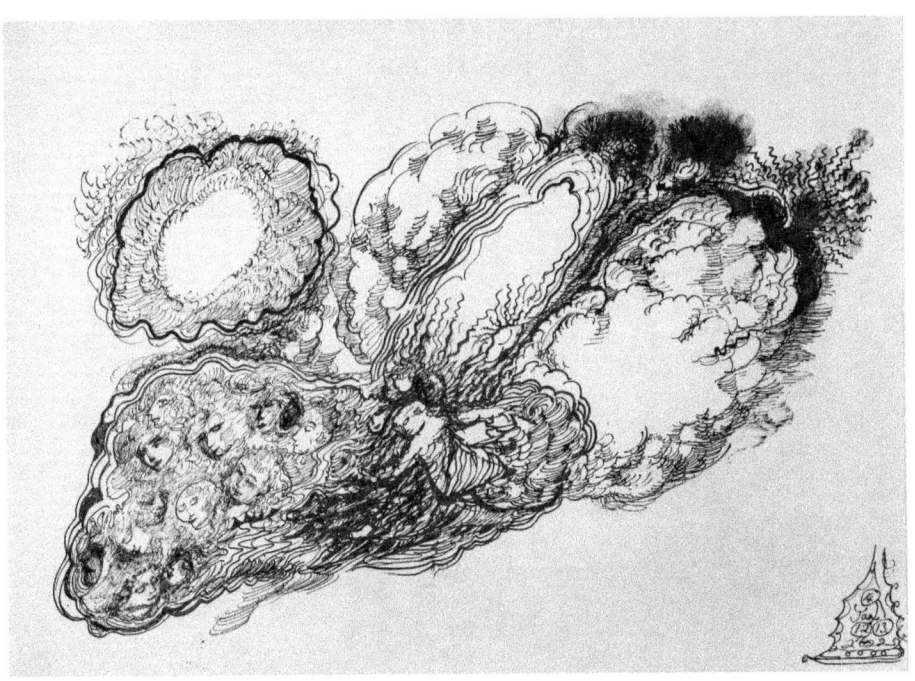

In an empty sky a small human flies forward. But it's unclear how, as the four wings appear composed of clouds. Three are empty apart from one with faces & profiles.

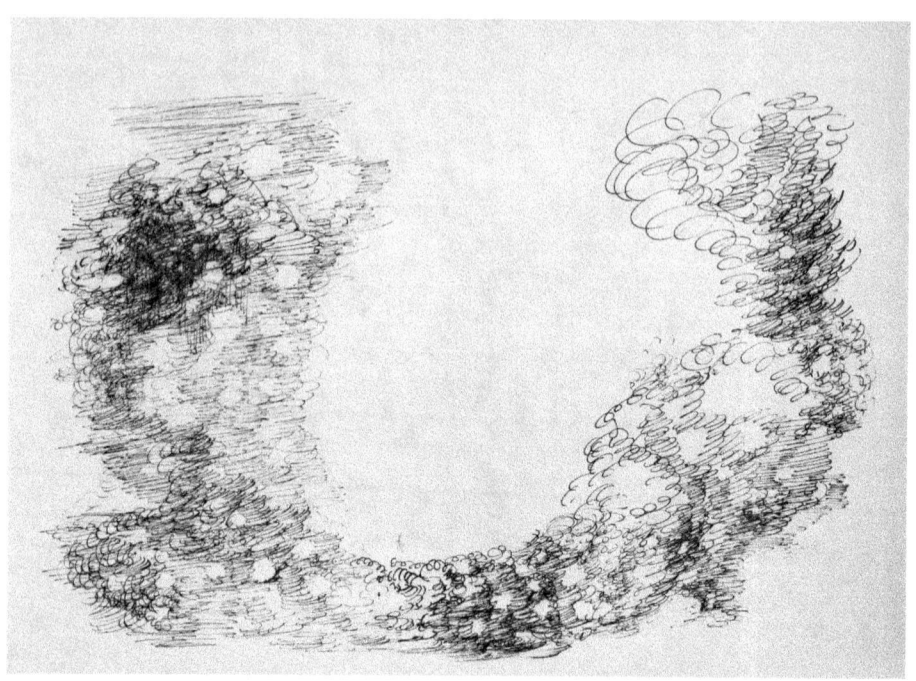

A page of empty sketched clouds, for the reader to draw or write in. I'd be interested to see what people put there.

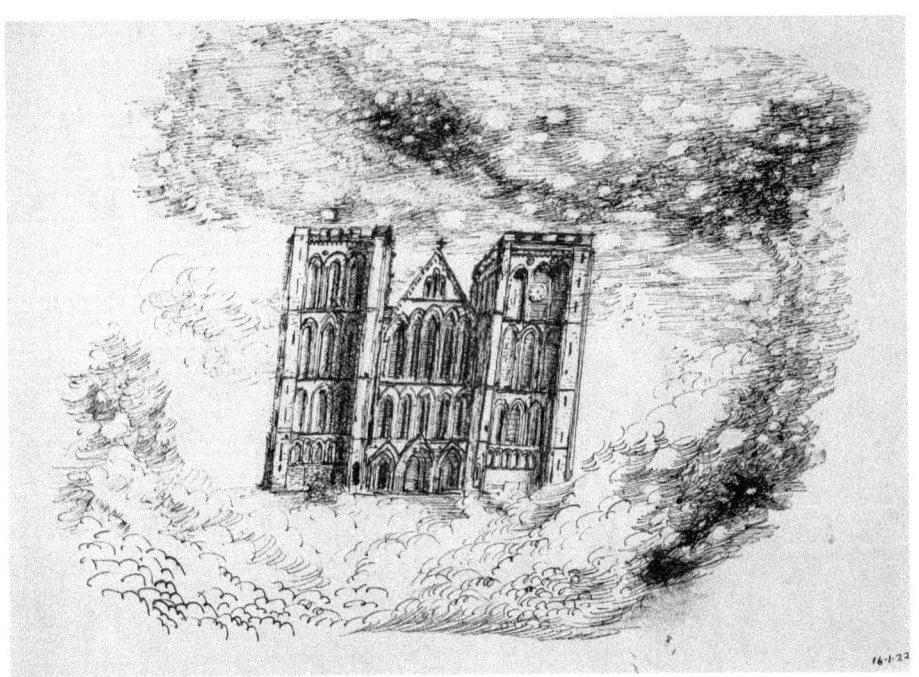

The west front of Ripon Cathedral, completed circa 1258 is notable for its rare Anglo Saxon origins & lancet windows ending in points. Founded by Irish Celtic monks from Melrose Abbey in 660 AD. Sacked by Danes in 875. Behind the 8 feet thick 1494 screen is a carved gryphon pursuing a rabbit, which could have inspired Lewis Carroll's Alice in Wonderland, whose father was a cannon there 1852 - 68.

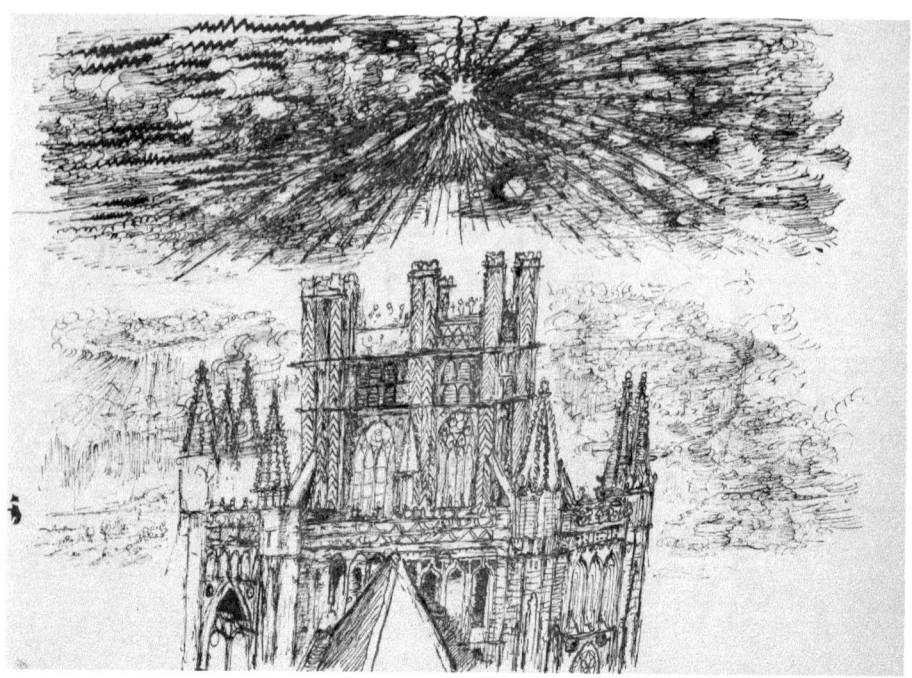

With origins in 672 AD. Ely Cathedral has an Octagon - a tower with high windows at the crossing of a cathedral so the light comes from far above. In European architecture Ely is unique. And what makes it so are the 63 ft long & 3'.6" giant vertical oak beams from Chicksands in Bedfordshire. Their outside is faced with lead.

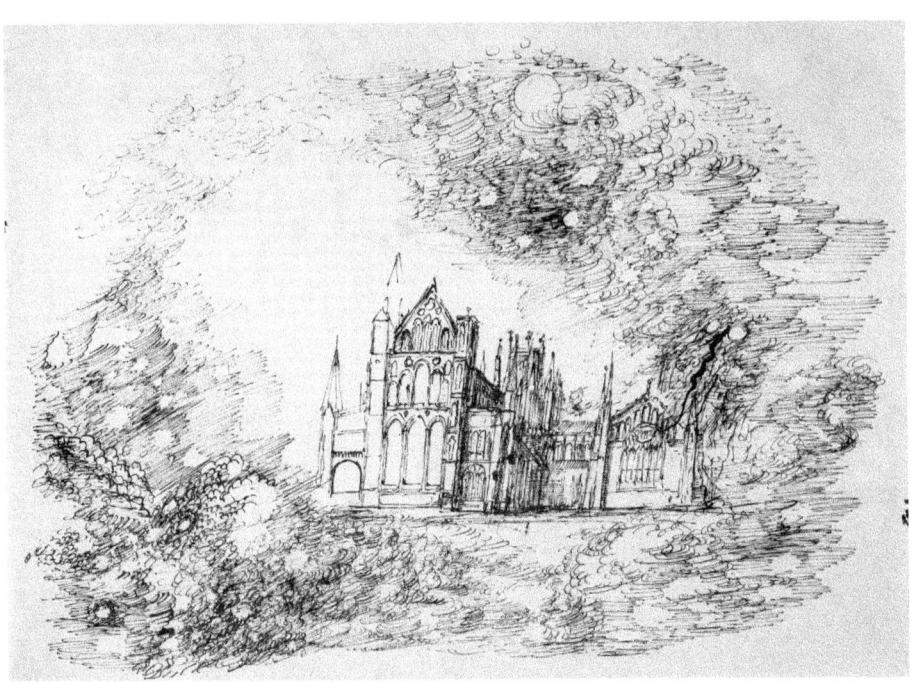

Ely Cathedral, in the Middle Ages called the 'Ship of the Fens' because the flatlands flooded & the people thought they saw her floating. Drawn in a swirling sky seen from the east is the Lady Chapel, the largest in the U.K. Lightning strikes.

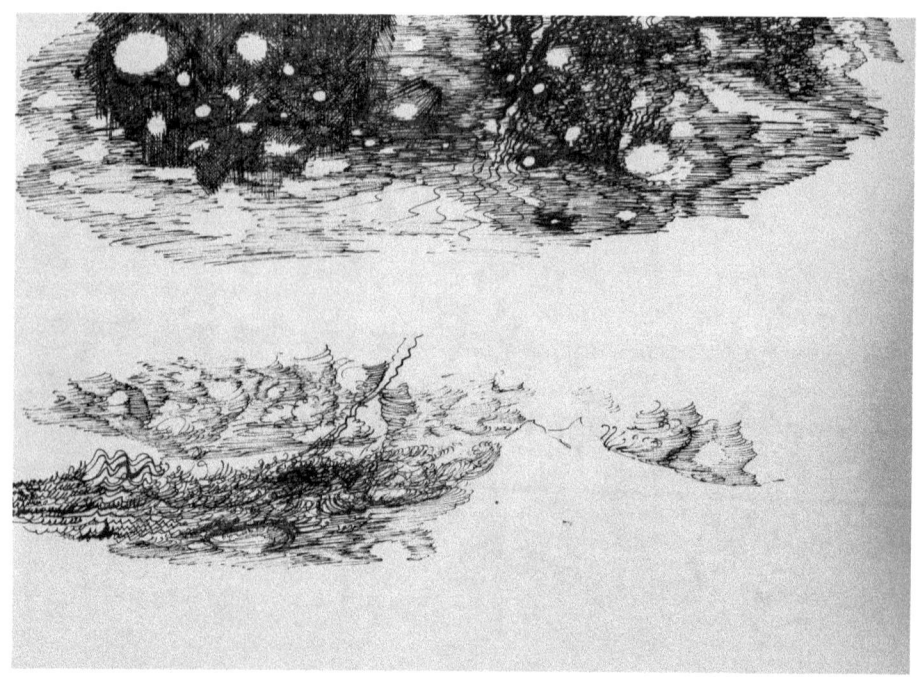

After a loud storm with thunder & lightning, a new horizon over the sea can be seen. What lies there?
Another book will follow soon.

Last comment

Many years ago I had an idea - to see the outside of a cathedral repainted in the bright colors it was when first built, making it visible from a great distance. We can't know those colors exactly, because time & the weather has washed them away, but wouldn't it be a dazzling sight to see the outside of just one painted again. Maybe someone with time & patience will overcome the bureaucracy & make it happen.

BOOKS BY THIS AUTHOR

The Year 2020 World In Chaos

Book has a colourful cover. The black & White drawings inside are based around nativities, nature, the surreal, & political caricatures. Some are recognisable or from other artists, Bible stories, & it features things like Astronomy & the Astrological Zodiac.

Although it's based on the Pandemic of 2020, the writing & style of the artworks have a timeless feel. The concise narrative works on several levels - in places it's informative about art history, at times it's direct & punchy, in others it's ambiguous.

The book questions our growing surveillance culture whereby the authorities can measure your face in one hundredth of a second & your gate/walk can also be measured by high resolution camera's relayed by 5G wi-fi, this ought to be queried more.

Digital money, cashless society is around the corner, the book does a good job of raising awareness.

The art in the book speaks for itself, you don't need me to preach how excellent it is, look at the eBook version free sample 35% peak inside & see the details page on Amazon.com - Deenagh Miller, The Year 2020 World in Chaos.

ABOUT THE AUTHOR

Deenagh Miller

Deenagh's life was fabulously dramatic until the age of thirty when she settled down & took painting & drawing seriously. Four decades creating high quality art has resulted.

Her home & studio is in Bristol near I.K. Brunel's famous Suspension Bridge. But lately she is found in Italy.

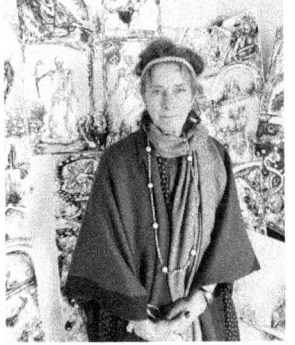

When she discovered her mother's art books as a child, books on Greek & Italian Renaissance art, Impressionist & Expressionist art & that of the 20th century she decided however long it took, she would be an artist herself.

Her son Peter is presently publishing a series of black & white drawings from the sketchbooks, drawn from the imagination, in a small, affordable format available on kindle, eBook & in print on demand.

EPILOGUE

Epilogue - 2 Quotes -

Edmund Burke, statesman, philosopher. 12 Jan 1729 - July 9 1797
'No man made a greater mistake than 'she or he' - who did nothing because 'he or she' could only do a little'.
An antidote to the anxiety & fear of standing out of the crowd.
For modernity I added the 'she'.

Fyodor Dostoyevsky, author, publisher. 11 Nov 1821 - Feb 9 1881
'Tolerance will reach a level that intelligent people will be banned from thinking so as not to offend the imbeciles'.
Remarkable prophecy.
Who are the imbeciles?